Inspired Celebrations

Inspired Celebrations

Easy Entertaining Ideas and Healthy Recipes for Everyday Life

Ngoc Nguyen Lay

Recipes by Tram Le, MS, RD
Photography by Caroline Tran

Brown Books Publishing Group
Dallas, Texas

© 2012 Ngoc Nguyen Lay

Inspired Celebrations
Easy Entertaining Ideas and Healthy Recipes for Everyday Life

Brown Books Publishing Group
16250 Knoll Trail, Suite 205
Dallas, Texas 75248
www.brownbooks.com
(972) 381-0009

ISBN 978-1-61254-065-8
Library of Congress Control Number 2012937450

Printed in the United States of America
10 9 8 7 6 5 4 3 2 1

For more information, please visit
www.InspiredCelebrationsBook.com
www.SkyboxEventProductions.com
www.CarolineTran.net
www.NutritionToKitchen.com

Contents

Left: Caroline Tran, Center: Ngoc Nguyen Lay, and Right: Tram Le

Acknowledgments

I would like to express my heartfelt thanks to all the people who have inspired me. Thank you to Tram and Caroline, who were the most incredible partners to work with on this extraordinary journey. Thank you to my dear husband, Albert Y. Lay, who has supported my every move—I love you! To my colleagues, friends, and family who have believed in me, thank you for making every day feel like a reason to celebrate!

—Ngoc Nguyen Lay

I wrote these recipes while recovering from a traumatic brain injury. Thank you, Mom, for all your help in the kitchen. I would also like to thank my mother-in-law for accompanying me on my path to healing. Thank you, Tiffany, for sampling my dishes. Thank you, Camille—you are my joy. Thank you, Ngoc, for including me in this project. Most importantly, thank you, Phong—I love you and could not have completed this journey without you.

—Tram Le

I would like to offer a huge thank-you to my biggest supporter, Jonathan, for making all of this possible, for taking care of everything before and after my photo shoots, and for feeding me! I honestly would not have been able to do any of this without you. I would like to send hugs and kisses to my baby, Cameron—I love it when you accompany me on photo shoots. It was wonderful having you along on the shoots for this book. Thank you to my mom and dad for their unwavering love and support. Last but not least, thank you, Ngoc, for our many adventures like this one!

—Caroline Tran

Introduction

The hour of your party is rapidly approaching and your guests are minutes away, but the food is nowhere near ready and the decorations aren't up yet. Does this situation sound familiar? Have you ever attended a get-together where the food tasted like leftovers and you thought that it was—dare I say it—a waste of time?

I have been a victim of those "this party couldn't possibly be any worse" blues. But what if I told you there was a way to make sure those blues never happen again? Many people believe that hosting a party requires more energy, creativity, and patience than they can muster. Not true! In this book we have gathered our favorite party planning tips just for you. We hope to inspire you to dream of the perfect celebration and to provide you with the essential planning tools to achieve that dream.

This book combines celebration ideas and easy recipes to create matches made in heaven. You can host the best events by following our inspirational advice for twelve different kinds of parties. This book offers specific, step-by-step instructions organized in a timeline fashion along with thematic ideas. Preparing an intimate dinner gathering for your closest friends or a large cocktail party doesn't have to be overwhelming. With the right tips and ideas it can be fun, exciting, and—once you get the hang of it—even easy. The recipes showcased in this book will not only appeal to your inner gourmand but are also easy and healthy. They will meet your needs for casual as well as sophisticated entertaining, and for light snacks as well as full meals.

Whether you are new to hosting parties or a veteran hostess looking for new ideas, we have you covered. With the tools we offer here, we aim to make your next party a success. The ultimate goal is to get it all done—and still have time to relax and enjoy your guests, because that's what the party is really about. Now let's have fun.

Part 1

The Essentials

one

The Basics

Planning your own party can be a daunting task. There are lots of decisions to make, plenty of details that require your attention, and a lot of people relying on your organizational skills. There is no need to fear, however—in this section you are provided with some professional tips that break down the process and make planning easier to manage. Before you begin your party planning, you need to know the basics.

Essential Party Planning Tips

Theme Basics

Determining the theme of your party is the first step to all planning. The theme is the tone or style you choose for the party. Everything from the invitations to the dessert should match the theme to give the party a cohesive feel. Your party's theme can be anything from elegant and formal to elegant and informal, from fun and low-key to fun and wild. Often the theme of the party will derive from the host's personality. If you are throwing a party for a child, you will want to match the theme to the personality and likes of the child. A kid's birthday party, for example, may employ a storybook character or favorite toy like a truck or boat for the theme. If you are having an adult cocktail party, connect the drinks to the theme: serve a variety of rum drinks for a Caribbean Island theme, or enjoy a Prohibition theme and ask people to dress in the fashions of the 1920s. Having a specific party theme might seem restrictive, but often it will actually start your creative juices flowing as you decide what type of invitation to send, what food to serve, and what music to play.

Some parties you throw, such as a bridal shower or engagement party, may not need a specific theme. Instead you should match the party's style to the personality of the guest of honor. Does she like pastels and floral patterns, or earth tones and adventurous activities? You can select decorations and party favors that match her personal style. For other parties, such as a movie night or Oktoberfest, the theme is contained in the event; you just have to decide how far you want to take it. Your options are endless: you can ask your guests to dress up or dress down; you can decorate to the hilt or have just a few accent decorations. You should always work with what your schedule and budget will allow.

Think about the theme that best suits your personality or the personality of the guest of honor, then let your imagination run wild. Don't worry if you have a tight budget: that's where being creative comes in. When you start planning early, you leave more room for creativity, finding deals, making your own decorations, or enlisting help.

Planning Basics

The real planning should begin immediately after your decision to have a party. Start by putting all your ideas down on paper. It is important to write things down so that you can stick to a plan. First, write down your budget. Under that, begin making a list of the main items that you will need to buy. Estimate the maximum you are willing to spend on each item and subtract that from the budget (see the sample Budget and Planning Form below). You may need to rework your list a few times after shopping around to research costs, but with a little advance planning and creativity you can

SAMPLE BUDGET AND PLANNING FORM

Budget: $1,250	Drinks: $150
Venue: $500	Music: $50
Invitations: $75	Decorations: $100
Food: $325	Party Favors: $50

make any budget work. To cut down on costs, maybe you could host the party in your home instead of renting a venue. You could also send evites instead of printed invitations, or make your own decorations or food instead of buying them premade. Determining your budget as a first step—and putting it down in writing—will help the rest of your planning go smoothly.

Deciding on the size of the party and which guests you will invite is another key element to early planning. These factors will help you determine where to hold your event. If your home can only comfortably host twenty-five people but you want to invite fifty, then you know you will need to find another venue. You may find that your budget greatly affects this aspect of the party. However, if you are creative in your brainstorming, you might be able to find an inexpensive alternative location that will allow you to host more people, such as an empty warehouse, a cleaned-out garage, or a friend's backyard. Consider the number of guests carefully, and try to invite people who do not know each other well. This will mix up the party's dynamic and keep things interesting.

Deciding where to have the party is a big factor. Renting space can be the greatest expense of the party. You will also have to consider the added cost and effort of transporting chairs and decorations, as well as either transporting the food to the location yourself or having it catered. For more formal affairs, such as an engagement party, a rented venue might be worth it, but for most parties your own home is the best way to go.

Once you have set the budget, guest list, and location down on paper, you can move from the initial planning stage to the doing stage. Next you must send invitations, choose and prepare the food and drinks, purchase the supplies, decorate the venue, and enjoy your party. Each of these basic steps requires a good deal of time and effort, even if it doesn't seem like it will. The key to pulling off a great party lies in the details. Consider asking someone for help with a few of these tasks. Take the process step-by-step, and work through problems as they arise. This way you should never find yourself overwhelmed.

Invitation Basics

There are a number of options open to you when it comes to invitations. You can either have them printed, print your own, or send them electronically. You should never text or Tweet your invitations; these methods are still too informal, even for today's modern age. If you decide to use electronic invitations, there are plenty of great online resources for invitation templates and RSVP management.

If you decide to use printed invitations then you will have to settle on a design. You can use a traditional invitation style, or opt for a more modern, creative, or even wacky design. Pay attention to the details and remember to match the invitations to the party's theme. Do not just throw something together with little effort, or your guests may expect you to do the same with your party. Take this opportunity to add an extra element of creativity to your party. Do something out of the ordinary with your invitations. Consider adding an appropriate photograph or work of art to the invitation. Maybe you could write the party details in rhyme. Use a special kind of paper or attach a ribbon or other embellishment, depending on the style of the party. Cut the invitations into the shape of something that matches the theme, such as a movie projector for a movie night (page 77), a sleeping bag for an overnight bash (page 87), an engagement ring for an engagement party (page 45), or a house for a housewarming party (page 69).

It is important to mail the invitations early enough so that people have time to plan accordingly. For most gatherings, you should send your invitations a minimum of two weeks before the party. Generally, you can assume that 10 percent of the people you invite will not be able to make it. This percentage may be a little higher for more formal parties. When you desire a higher percentage of acceptances for a formal gathering, consider sending your invitations as much as eight weeks in advance. Some people schedule their lives very tightly and will need the extra time to plan.

Food and Drink Basics

When planning the food for your party you will need to consider whether your guests will expect a full meal or simply light snacks. The general principle is that if your party is held over the conventional lunch hour (12:00 p.m.) or dinner hour (6:30 p.m.), then you should provide more than just a few snacks. If your party is scheduled between meals, you can get away with serving a few snacks and perhaps a cake, when appropriate.

SNACKS OR MEAL?

Party Times	Foods to Serve
10:00 a.m.–12:00 p.m.	**Snacks are fine:** chips, nuts, cake, soda, coffee, tea
10:00 a.m.–2:00 p.m.	**Meal is required:** sandwiches, pizza, substantial finger food, soda, iced tea
2:00 p.m.–4:00 p.m.	**Snacks are fine:** chips, nuts, hors d'oeuvres, alcoholic or nonalcoholic drinks
4:00 p.m.–6:00 p.m.	**Snacks are fine:** chips, nuts, hors d'oeuvres, finger food, alcoholic or nonalcoholic drinks
6:00 p.m.–8:00 p.m.	**Meal is required:** hors d'oeuvres, substantial finger food, petite sandwiches, a sit-down dinner if desired, desserts, alcoholic or nonalcoholic drinks
8:00 p.m.–10:00 p.m.	**Snacks are fine:** chips, nuts, hors d'oeuvres, finger food, alcoholic or nonalcoholic drinks

The type of food you provide will also depend on whether you plan to have your party catered or to handle the food yourself. If you do not plan to cater, you need to determine how much food you are willing to prepare at home and how much you will buy premade. A caterer will provide you with a list of hors d'oeuvres and snacks from which to choose. These will typically be divided into price tiers based on the expense of the ingredients and the difficulty of preparation. The Russian caviar and chèvre-stuffed dates will cost more than hummus and a simple cheese plate. You will need to work with the caterer to determine the right selection for your theme, budget, and number of guests.

If you do not want to use a full-service caterer, but neither are you interested in spending much time in the kitchen, consider supplementing a few of your signature homemade appetizers with some store-bought items. Warehouse stores such as Smart & Final, Costco, and Sam's Club carry a wonderful assortment of great-tasting party foods such as miniature quiches, dips, chicken wings, miniature cheesecakes, cream puffs, and the like. You can also serve bowls of nuts, sesame sticks, miniature nonpareils,

SNACK GUIDE

This chart assumes one 12-ounce bag of chips, sixteen ounces of dip, and one 9-inch cake. You should provide at least three pieces of finger food (e.g., meatballs, pinwheels, cookies, etc.) per person.

Number of People	Number of Snacks	Food Ideas
0–10	3 kinds	Chips and dip, nuts or fruit, cake
10–15	4 kinds	Add another dip or nachos
15–20	5 kinds	Add pinwheels or cookies
20–25	6 kinds	Add meatballs or pigs in a blanket
25+	7 kinds	Add stuffed olives or bacon-wrapped dates

and jelly beans. Such items can be purchased for a reasonable price from the bulk bins at most grocery stores. If you are hosting a more formal sit-down dinner and are on a tight budget, consider asking guests to bring some side dishes to help alleviate cost and effort.

When deciding how much food to prepare, you need to consider both the number of guests and the length of the party. When serving snacks as opposed to a meal, you should try to have a minimum of three different options for a party of up to ten guests. For every five additional guests, add another type of snack until you have six or seven different options. Gauging the amount of each snack is a little trickier. It is safer to err on the side of too much rather than too little. If you think one bag of chips or nuts it is probably enough, go ahead and get two. If you are not sure whether one batch of cookies is enough, bake two. You can always freeze the leftovers.

Meal Guide

This chart assumes side dishes and main dishes that serve four to six people. When you are preparing a meal for a crowd, it can be difficult to estimate serving sizes, especially for the main dishes. Keep in mind that it is best to plan on about eight ounces of meat per person for a main dish. This should ensure there is enough for some people to have seconds. If you are having pasta as a main dish, supply another vegetable side rather than a starch, or serve a salad with the pasta.

Number of People	Number of Sides	Number of Main Dishes
0–10	3	1
10–15	3–4	1–2
15–20	4–5	1–2
20–25	5–6	2
25+	6	2–3

When planning the drinks for your party, you must consider the crowd as well as the time of the party. If you are having an early afternoon birthday party for older kids and know that the adults will enjoy beer and wine, it is fine to have a few bottles of each on hand for your guests. However, do not worry about having a fully stocked bar since the adults are not the focus of the party.

When you are planning an evening affair for adults only, having a properly stocked bar is important (see page 38 for tips on stocking a bar for a cocktail party). The amount of beverages to have on hand again depends on the number of people. For both alcoholic and nonalcoholic drinks, plan to provide one beverage per person per hour. Assume that 40 percent of your guests drink beer, 30 percent prefer hard liquor, and 30 percent sip wine.

HOW MUCH LIQUOR TO BUY

The following is a general guide based on moderate drinkers. Adjust the list if you know your guests tend to be light drinkers, or enjoy a particular kind of beverage. Mixers include sodas, tonic water, soda water, fruit juices, and specialty mixes like piña colada. *Keep in mind that the mixers should be varied, such as 2-liters of sodas, ginger-ale, tonic water, various juices, and specialty mixes like piña colada.*

	10 People	25 People	50 People	100 People
Beer	24 bottles	60 bottles	120 bottles	240 bottles
Wine and Champagne	4 bottles	9 bottles	18 bottles	36 bottles
Hard liquor	2 bottles	3 bottles	6 bottles	11 bottles
Mixers	4 liters	12 liters	24 liters	48 liters

Entertainment and Activities Basics

Your entertainment choices will depend on the nature of your party. The socializing at a cocktail party or the movie at an outdoor movie night will serve as the central entertainment of these parties. A birthday party for kids will require structured activities and entertainment to keep the young ones occupied. When you throw a party for kids under the age of approximately sixteen, it is always good to have some games and activities planned. Try to have enough of an assortment of games and activities to occupy all the children in attendance. If you have ten kids at the party, you will need to have more than one gaming device with only two controllers on hand. Make several age-appropriate board games available, or plan some activities and take the lead in setting them up and getting the kids involved. Here are some activities that almost all kids can enjoy:

- Pilgrim Voyage
  Pick a child to be "The New World" and sit on a chair on one side of the room. Pick another child to be "The Mayflower" and stand at the other side of the room. Blindfold "The Mayflower." Have the other children be icebergs by sitting on the floor between the two. Have "The New World" direct "The Mayflower" through the sea of children to the chair.

- Marble Roll
  Place an empty shoe box open side down and cut five upside-down V-shaped notches into the long side. Make the middle notch just a little larger than the marbles and the outer notches up to twice as large. Number the wider holes with a 3, the medium holes with a 4, and the smallest hole with a 5. Roll the marbles from three to six feet away and keep score.

- Crazy Catch
  Write on several strips of masking tape different rules for throwing a ball, such as standing on one foot, throwing the ball underhanded, or throwing it with your eyes closed. Stick the tape strips onto one large ball. Whoever catches the ball has to follow the rule closest to his or her left thumb.

Keep the sensitivities of your guests in mind when you are deciding on entertainment. You probably do not want to hire a nightclub DJ for a middle school graduation party, and your bridal shower guests may not want to spend their entire afternoon making cutesy crafts. There is a plethora of online resources for game ideas for various parties. Most adult parties will not require much entertainment planning beyond good music to provide ambience. Since people's tastes vary widely when it comes to music and the options are endless, it never hurts to solicit suggestions—or even borrow CDs or MP3s—from some of your guests when creating the playlist for your party. If you want to provide some easy and entertaining activities for adults, here are some options to consider:

- Icebreaker Bingo
  The host provides a Bingo-style game sheet with a specific fact about each guest inside each square. The guests must mingle, asking questions to determine which trait goes with which guest in order to mark off each square.

- Needs a Name
  The host passes out pieces of paper to the guests and instructs them to write down one funny and random fact about themselves without revealing their identity. After collecting all the papers, the host reads each fact aloud. The guests must guess which person belongs to each fact.

- Curses
  The host writes a curse for each guest on a note card. Each guest draws a card when they arrive, and then must live under the curse for the rest of the party. Curses can include things like "must talk like a pirate," "may only use the left hand," or "cannot use the words drink, pass, or what."

Supplies Basics

There are certain items you will need for just about any party, such as plates, cups, cutlery, napkins, trash cans, and table coverings. Style and quantity are the variables when it comes to these supplies. If you are having a themed or informal party, paper plates and cups are fine, and a plastic table covering might be just right. For more formal parties, elegant clear plastic plates, cups, and cutlery along with linen tablecloths are probably in order. So how many plates and cups do you need? If you serve finger food as well as cake, you should provide at least two plates for every person. Always buy extra cutlery and cups, as people tend to misplace these or throw them away. For children's parties, remember that the adults will be eating and drinking too.

For a child's birthday party with finger food and cake	
Number of People	Number of Supplies
8 people	16 plates, 16 napkins, 12 cups, 12 forks
10 people	20 plates, 20 napkins, 15 cups, 15 forks
15 people	30 plates, 30 napkins, 20 cups, 20 forks
20 people	40 plates, 40 napkins, 30 cups, 30 forks

When the drinks are the main focus of the party, such as at a cocktail party, you should provide far more cups than you do plates. Remember that people may want to try different drinks, and they will need a new cup each time. Keep in mind that you will need as many cocktail napkins as cups, but don't worry about having dinner napkins as well if all you plan to serve is finger food.

For an adult party with finger food and adult beverages	
Number of People	Number of Supplies
8 people	16 plates, 24 cocktail napkins, 24 cups
10 people	20 plates, 30 cocktail napkins, 30 cups
15 people	30 plates, 45 cocktail napkins, 45 cups
20 people	40 plates, 60 cocktail napkins, 60 cups

If you are having a sit-down dinner party, you will probably want to bring out your fine china. If you do not have enough plates for salads as well as desserts, consider soliciting some help to wash the small plates between courses.

Other supplies to consider are serving tables. A formal buffet arrangement is great for a sit-down dinner party and can even work for cocktail parties or bridal showers. For a child's birthday party or a movie night, a simple folding table covered with a tablecloth will often do the trick. It is always important to ensure your guests will have easy access to the food. When possible, it is best to allow for access from both sides of the serving table.

For many parties you will want to purchase decorations and party favors as well. It is a good idea to begin buying these items early to allow yourself enough time to find just the right decorations and favors, take advantage of deals, and leave time for assembling any gift bags or centerpieces.

Decorating Basics

Decorating your party does not have to be a chore. Decide early in your planning process how much decorating you are willing to do. When you are out purchasing your supplies, you may see something that will add flair to your event. Try to stick with a few simple decorating ideas. You can always fill in the gaps as the party comes together.

Basic Decorating Ideas

- Banners
  Printing a celebratory message on a banner adds a fun touch to any party. You can make your own at home or order one from a local print shop or office supply store.

- Bows
  Make large bows out of ribbons and attach them to the backs of chairs, or tie small bows around serving pitchers or candles. Little touches like this can make a big difference.

- Balloons

  The theme of the party will often determine the color of the balloons. Buy a dozen white and silver balloons for an engagement party, or some black and gold ones for a cocktail party. Get a dozen colored ones in various sizes for a kid's birthday party or a movie night. Balloons are an easy way to add a festive touch.

- Candles

  Lighting candles around the house adds a soft ambience to a party. Self-contained jar candles are safe and easy, or you could opt for a floating candle arrangement. Use scented candles in the bathroom to provide a warm, aromatic presence. However, for parties with many children in attendance, use real candles only on a birthday cake. There is no sense in risking a fire.

- Centerpieces

  Every party needs a centerpiece on the table where the food is served. The centerpiece does not have to be elaborate, but it should complement the food being served. It can be anything from a simple votive candle floating in a bowl of water or a simple flower arrangement to a more complex arrangement of flowers, candles, and greenery or even a diorama matching your party's theme.

- Streamers

  If you have a tall ceiling, the use of streamers is a good way to utilize this space for decoration. If you have a tall ladder, attach the streamers along the edges of the ceiling and bring them down to a center point over the serving table.

- Toppers

  Food toppers are a fun addition to a party. For finger food, consider buying some festive toothpicks that match your party's theme. Any party store should carry a variety of decorative toothpicks.

Once you have the basics down, you might consider some extra accents that turn up along the way. For instance, you already have the balloons, streamers, and banner for your child's sports-themed birthday party. Then, a few days before the party, you see some soccer ball straws on sale. A dozen of those might add that last special touch.

Or maybe you have all your bridal shower supplies lined up when you find the frosted champagne flutes that will be perfect for a toast over the Amaretto cake. Or, after planning a movie night, you stumble upon some ticket stub invitations that would be perfect. As you begin to pull the party together, you will think of these little accents that add a nice touch and make the party your own.

Relaxing Basics

One of the hardest aspects of the party is remembering to relax and enjoy yourself when you are playing the host or hostess. Unless you thrive on stress and can look calm while managing many things, the only way to truly relax is to solicit some help. Do not be afraid or embarrassed to ask your friends for a little help with some of the tasks. Ask a friend to monitor the food and drinks. Let her know where extra snacks, appetizers, and beverages are kept. Ask an adolescent to monitor the trash cans—just let him know where to put the trash bags when they are full and where to find new bags. If you plan activities, enlist the help of a friend to pass out supplies or act as a referee. Making someone else responsible for a little task will not stop them from enjoying your party. When you have a few people helping, you will find a huge load is off you.

A HELPING HAND

	Task	Description	Assigned to
☐	Activities	Help prepare and direct activities	
☐	Bussing	Throw away used plates and cups	
☐	Bathrooms	Refill toilet paper and soap, ensure overall cleanliness	
☐	Greeting	Open the door and welcome guests, take their coats, if applicable	
☐	Refills	Refill serving trays and punch bowls with prepared food	
☐	Trash	Remove full trash bags and replace with new ones	

The key to your party's success is careful planning, creativity, and a little bit of help. Then you can relax and enjoy the fruit of your efforts with your guests. The party planning process can seem overwhelming when you think of everything that has to be done, but just follow the basic tips and remember to take things one step at a time. Mark a calendar with the tasks you need complete by a certain date. Spreading out the tasks over a longer period of time will make them more manageable. In the next section you will find ideas for specific parties. Keep in mind these essentials and let your imagination take care of the rest.

Part 2

The Parties

two

Birthday

Watch your daughter's eyes light up as she steps into the fantasy world of a royal tea party. The room overflows with jewelry, flowers, and teacups. She will be caught up in the moment. A themed birthday party like this one uses some relatively easy decorations and activities to make the event come alive.

Birthdays are a special time for the one being honored. Everyone loves to be celebrated by family and friends. Although this section focuses on a young child's birthday, the same basic principles can be applied to birthday parties for people of all ages. For an adult birthday party, you may want to incorporate some of the elements of the cocktail party found on page 33.

Pick a Theme

Four to Five Weeks Before the Party

Reread the section Theme Basics (page 1) to explore some different themes for your party. Older children may want an action hero or princess theme. Younger children enjoy bright, bold colors in a theme. Whether you decide on an elaborate Royal Tea Party theme, a storybook theme, or simply center your party around your child's favorite color, selecting a theme will help you organize your thoughts. (See the Royal Tea Party–themed party photo on the opposite page.) Then plan all of your party supply purchases—including invitations, decorations, and food—around that theme. The theme lays the foundation for all the other decisions you will need to make. Once you have settled on your theme, you are ready to start planning the party.

Stylist: Linda Ly, Grand Soirées Event Design & Coordination

Plan the Party

Four Weeks Before the Party

It is a good idea to begin planning your party at least four weeks in advance. This will allow plenty of time for online shopping, cake orders, and enlisting the help of friends or family. As you plan, keep in mind that children remember what they did at a party much more than what they ate, what the plates and napkins looked like, or whether the house was spotless. Don't sweat the cleaning details!

At this stage of planning there are three main things you need to do. First, you need to decide on the timing of your party. For parties of young, school-age children, the best party times are generally from 1:00 to 3:00 p.m., or from 2:00 to 4:00 p.m. When younger children are involved, it is a good idea to plan the party between 10:00 and 11:30 a.m. to work around nap times.

The second thing you must do is decide how many people to invite. If the party is for children under eight years old, consider this invitation equation: child's age + one = happy party. For children under the age of eight, invite as many kids as the child's age plus one. Some parents choose to add an extra guest or two to this equation. Only you can know the limits of yourself and your child. Of course, as your child gets older he or she will want to be more involved in the process of selecting guests.

This equation is just a guideline. Consider the space you have to work with as well as your own personal limits. Some people thrive on the chaos created by a large group of children, but others can feel overwhelmed by having just a few children in their home and will want to keep the party on the small side.

The third thing you need to do is determine whom you will invite. Parties for very young children are often made up of close family members: siblings, cousins, aunts, and uncles. As your child gets older, invite only your child's closest playmates. They already know each other well, which makes the party much more fun and can cut down on squabbles. Other people you may want to consider inviting are friends from daycare or school, relatives, and neighbors.

It is not mandatory for you to invite the siblings of your child's friends, or even the friends' parents, unless children are very young. Most parents enjoy the break that your party will provide, and you will avoid the pressure of entertaining the adults as well as the children. It is also not mandatory that you invite everyone in your child's class. If you feel the need to include everyone in the class, ask the teacher if you can come to the school for a brief and simple class party. Bring small party bags with favors (pencils, stickers, or balloons) and simple treats (cookies, cupcakes, or brownies) for every student.

Send the Invitations

Three Weeks Before the Party

Once you have your date, time, and guest list set, you need to choose the invitations and determine how they will complement the party's theme. If you are having a storybook party, for example, you should choose invitations that match that theme, such as invitations with bears on them for *Goldilocks and the Three Bears* or invitations with pink pigs for a *Three Little Pigs* party. For our Royal Tea Party theme, we chose an elegant card invitation with a silhouette on the front cover and a graceful script set within an oval border on the inside:

HOW TO MAKE ROYAL TEA PARTY INVITATIONS

1. If you are comfortable with a computer, create your invitation in a word processing program. Print the inside of the card, then run it through the printer again for the front cover. If you are not handy with a computer, you can make your card by hand and use simple scrapbooking embellishments, which can found at any craft store.

2. To make the silhouette, use a photo of your child's profile. Using tracing paper, trace the outline of the profile. Tape the tracing paper to a piece of black construction paper and cut along the outline.

3. Glue the silhouette onto the front and inside of your card. Take the card to a copy store along with your card stock and have a technician help you print the cards on both sides.

4. Fold each card in half.

Depending on the formality of your party and the nature of your theme, you can either mail your invitations or send electronic invitations by e-mail. There are a number of great electronic invitation resources available for free online. Just ensure that your invitations match your theme. And remember, even if you are throwing a party for older kids, you should never text an invitation to a party, no matter how tempting this might be.

Ask your guests to RSVP by one week before the party. If you are sending electronic invitations or using an e-vite service, RSVPs are usually handled automatically online. If you send paper invitations, consider setting up a designated e-mail address for your RSVPs and remember to check it regularly.

Choose the Cake and Snacks

Three Weeks Before the Party

You will not know exactly how many people will attend the party at this point, but it is important to order the cake and line up a caterer ahead of time. Although you may end up with fewer guests than you invited, it is good to be prepared and have enough food for everyone. If you want to make your own cake and snacks, then you will not need

to begin assembling these things until about a week before your party. In our Royal Tea Party example, we chose to hire a professional cake decorator to add the silhouette image from the invitations to the top of the cake. As an alternative, if you are artistic, see the instructions for the Royal Tea Party Cake on page 29.

Collect Supplies and Decorations

Two Weeks Before the Party

Once you have your theme and cake planned, you should begin thinking about your decorations. Now is the time to start looking around for supplies and decorations that will match your theme. You will need to buy the basics, including napkins, plates, cups, and tablecloths. While you are shopping for these items, look for inexpensive store-bought decorations. For a Royal Tea Party, for example, look for bows for girls, bow ties for boys, inexpensive costume jewelry, ribbons, fancy straws, or flower bouquets. Collect as many appropriately themed supplies as you can. You can also use these in the centerpiece or as party favors.

Decide on Games and Activities

Two Weeks Before the Party

If you begin planning your games and activities early, you will have time to collect any props or materials you will need. During this process, you may find that a particular game or activity is too difficult to pull off. Starting early allows you time to adjust your plans.

A party should be fun. Avoid tears by structuring games so that everyone has a chance to succeed. For example, if you plan a game like musical chairs, in which a player can be "called out," assign that player the task of playing the music. Every child who is eliminated gets to play DJ for the next round. After the game ends, all the players can rejoin the group for the next game. Another option is to plan a few cooperative games, in which the whole gang faces a challenge together, such as following a map to find hidden treasure. Each child can receive a prize, or the treasure can be split evenly at the game's end.

For a storybook party, you can make your own variations on traditional games. For instance, at a *Three Little Pigs* party, playing Pig, Pig, Wolf is much more fun than plain old Duck, Duck, Goose. It is wonderful if you can find or make up games that match the party's theme, but do not allow your theme to become a constraint.

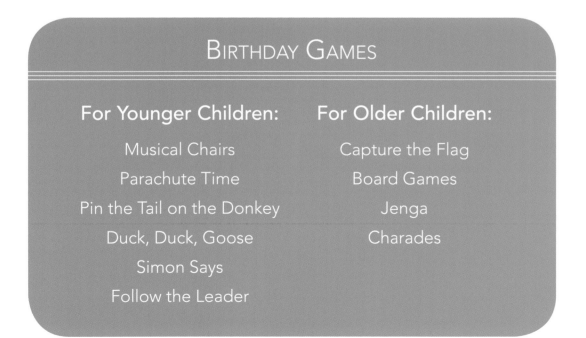

BIRTHDAY GAMES

For Younger Children:

Musical Chairs

Parachute Time

Pin the Tail on the Donkey

Duck, Duck, Goose

Simon Says

Follow the Leader

For Older Children:

Capture the Flag

Board Games

Jenga

Charades

Activity stations are a great way to ensure that all the children enjoy themselves. These stations can include activities like making stickers, cutting out silhouettes, making hats, applying nail polish, and decorating ice cream cups. Each child can pick what he or she wants to do. You should not need more than four stations. Ask a friend, family member, or neighbor to help with this aspect of the party. There may be a teenager in your neighborhood who would love to help. You can even offer them a few dollars for their time. Be sure to prepare all of the activities and games before the party. This will allow you to focus on the kids when the party begins.

Select the Party Favors

One Week Before the Party

When choosing party favors, it's better to spend more creativity than money. Give a wonderful "thank you for coming" item that reflects the party theme: a flowerpot and seeds for a garden party, modeling clay for an art party. You can even send the kids home with a treasure they made during the party. The birthday child should hand out the favors as a way to say "thank you" to his or her guests.

PARTY FAVORS FOR A ROYAL TEA PARTY

Pick a few of these items and put them in a fabric bag that you have decorated to match the theme of the party, perhaps using the silhouette of your daughter or a colored ribbon:

Faux pearl necklaces
Blue silk bows
Blue crystal bracelets
Bow ties
Paper crowns

Crayons
Coloring books
Ribbon wands
Snacks
Bubbles

Decorate Your House

Three Days Before the Party

It is a good idea to take inventory of what you have bought and accomplished and what you still need to do a few days before the party. This gives you time to begin working on any of the more complicated decorations. For example, for a Royal Tea Party you could make a wooden sign to post in front of your house. Arrange your tables and chairs and set out centerpieces and candles ahead of time. Remember that it is best to use flameless candles for a child's party. Try to get as much of the decorating done as early as possible.

How to Make a Wooden Tea House Sign

1. Cut a 28"x12" or 2'x16" board into one 12"x12" piece and one 12"x16" piece.
2. Cut the corners off the 12"x16" piece as shown above.
3. Paint your child's name on the 12"x12" piece and glue the cut piece on top to form the room.
4. Attach some balloons to the top of the sign and place on your mailbox or in your front yard.

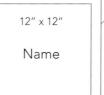

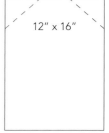

Make the Cake and Snacks

One Day Before the Party

If you have decided to purchase a cake, you should plan to pick it up the day before your party so that you will have time to fix any problems that might arise. Be sure to let your bakery know when you plan to pick it up. If you decide to make your own cake, it is still a good idea to make it the day before to free you up for last-minute preparations.

How to Make a Royal Tea Party Cake

1. Bake one 9-inch round cake following a favorite recipe. Let it cool.
   (See page 6 to determine the amount of cake you will need.)
2. Cover the top and sides of the cake with white frosting.
3. Use the tracing paper from the invitations to cut out a reverse template on parchment paper. Place the parchment paper over the top of the cake.
4. With black frosting, copy the silhouette of your child onto the top of the cake.
5. With light blue frosting, draw an oval border on top of the cake. Write "Happy Birthday" above the silhouette and your child's name below.

Most snacks can be made a couple days in advance. Try to provide finger food that is simple, easy to eat, and will be liked by even the pickiest of eaters. For our Royal Tea Party we focused on pinwheel sandwiches. Also consider providing some other treats such as cookies, brownies, cucumber sandwiches, peanut butter and jelly sandwiches, and cinnamon and sugar toast.

FINGER FOOD IDEAS

Pigs in a Blanket
(page 170)

Chicken Nuggets
(page 168)

Bacon-Wrapped Dates
(page 155)

Stuffed Olives

Cookie Dough Bites
(page 214)

Chocolate Chip Cookies

Vegetables and
Sour Cream Dip
(page 162)

Pita Chips and White Bean Dip
(page 159)

Guacamole
(page 156)

Pizza Pinwheels
(page 162)

Trail Mix
(page 171)

Last-Minute Preparations

The Night Before or Morning of the Party

The morning of the party day will be the busiest time for you as you attend to all the final touches. Place the wooden tea house sign in your front yard. Pick up a handful of helium balloons to decorate the house and the sign. If you are using your own balloons, now is the time to blow them up (you should have about twenty-five per 200-square-foot room). Attach them to furniture and other fixtures in the rooms where the party will be held. Be sure to use an indiscreet painter's tape that will not damage any surfaces.

Put out the tablecloths and centerpieces and organize the activity stations. The house should be ready to go one hour before your party's start time. This will allow you time to get yourself ready, take care of any last-minute issues, and then relax. About ten minutes before the guests arrive, double-check all the food and drinks. Everything should be ready and in place as your guests begin to arrive.

Remember to have fun and enjoy the celebration of your child's birth!

- three -

Cocktail Party

Cocktail parties are a great way for adults to mingle. They are suitable for almost any occasion, can be elegant or simple, and are appropriate for casual social gatherings and work functions alike. With the right planning tips, decorating suggestions, and food ideas, even a cocktail party for a group of thirty people will be easily within your reach.

Pick a Theme

Four to Five Weeks Before the Party

Picking a theme for your cocktail party does not have to be a challenge—just go with what you like. If you are a laid-back person, you may want to make use of some gentle lighting and play soft jazz or classical music to help set the mood for the party. If you are more energetic, you may prefer to provide pop music, colorful lights, and a place for people to dance. Or you can decide to do something more elaborate and go with a certain theme, transforming your party venue into a tropical island or a 1920s speakeasy. In the following example, however, the party is simple and the main focus is on the cocktails.

Stylist: Carolyn Chen, The Special Day

DRESSING THE PART

Cocktail parties traditionally have a semiformal dress code. Stylish clothing and accessories are a must for the guests of such a young, savvy affair. Make sure to include dress code instructions on your invitations so that your guests will know what to expect.

Plan the Party

Four Weeks Before the Party

Most cocktail parties begin between 8:00 and 10:00 p.m. Your party's start time will depend on how late your friends stay up. Unlike other parties that occur in the afternoon or evening, there is typically no official end time for cocktail parties. You will need to gauge the energy and engagement of your crowd.

As you decide whom to invite, it is important to consider people's temperaments (avoid inviting obnoxious drunks), relationships with each other (avoid inviting hostile exes), and whether the people you invite already know each other. Inviting a variety of people from different parts of your life can encourage guests to mingle and keep conversation lively.

The right location of your cocktail party helps set the mood. For a cozy affair, such as the cocktail party for eight that is described here, your living area may work fine. For a larger gathering, you could consider an outdoor patio or poolside setting, or even rent a small ballroom. Whatever the size of the party, you should keep the comfort of your guests in mind. Make sure there is plenty of room to move, and be sure to provide adequate seating.

Send the Invitations

Four Weeks Before the Party

When it comes to your cocktail party, the invitations are the first thing your guests will see. They will set the tone for the party. Choose an invitation design that matches the theme of your party. For an elegant gathering, use decorative script and gold lettering. For a reggae theme, use a red, yellow, and green color scheme. Be sure the invitation specifies the dress code and gives the party guests an idea of what to expect, such as mentioning whether food will be served. Remember to provide your contact information so that guests can RSVP. For an informal cocktail party, e-mail or electronic invitations are fine.

A MODERN CHIC–THEMED INVITATION

A Modern Chic Cocktail Affair

You are cordially invited to a cocktail party
hosted by Jannie Nelson

When: 9:00 p.m.

Where: The Nelson Manor at 2300 Moss Lane, NY 34906

Dress: Smart Causal

RSVP: By e-mail to host@events.com, or by
phone at (303) 555-1010, by June 10

Weather permitting, an outdoor buffet will be served.
In the case of rain, we will use the grand ballroom
in the main house.

Choose the Food

Three Weeks Before the Party

Since cocktail parties usually begin long after the traditional dinner hour, you will only need to serve a light amount of food. Keep in mind that if you are hiring a caterer for this event, it may be necessary to call six weeks ahead of time. If you plan to make the food yourself, keep it simple, but make sure you have plenty of appetizers. If your guests are drinking on an empty stomach, your elegant cocktail party could quickly become a "drink-a-thon."

Be sure to select food and drinks that match your theme. By setting your menu early you will ensure you have plenty of time to shop around for the best deals and best quality. It is best to serve a variety of snacks with both protein and starch, both to complement the drinks and give any guests who have not eaten dinner something substantial to snack on.

COCKTAIL FOODS

Cheese Plates	Salsas
Fruit Plates	Nuts
Chips and Dips	Asian-Inspired Meatballs (page 176)
Mini Quiches	
Shrimp and Edamame Lettuce Cups (page 160)	Earl Grey Tea Cookies (pages 216)
	Mini Cheesecakes
Shrimp Skewers (page 171)	Mini Pastries

Choose the Drinks and Cocktails

Three Weeks Before the Party

Cocktail parties require more thought and effort when it comes to the drinks than other parties do. Decide ahead of time what drinks you will be serving, and have several lists drawn up for guests to look at. Restricting the number of spirits you use will make the bartender's job easier.

Make sure you have all the equipment you will need to make the specific cocktails before the party starts. A well-stocked bar has a good amount of ice, plenty of cocktail glasses, the right mixers, some garnishes, and a lot of napkins (see the advice for stocking a bar on page 38 for more information). Make sure you have some help to collect and wash glasses periodically. Drink charms are helpful way for people to keep track of their glasses, and they will reduce the number of glasses used.

You should always have some nonalcoholic drinks available for those who are not drinking alcohol. These can include the mixers—such as soda or juice—water, or nonalcoholic beer. Have a contingency plan for guests who consume a little too much. Either request designated drivers, provide a taxi service, or be prepared to accommodate guests if they have no other way to get home.

HOW TO STOCK A BAR

	Basic	Add for Well Stocked	Add for Fully Stocked
Liquors	Vodka	Tequila	Coconut Rum
	Rum	Gin	Flavored Vodka
	Bourbon	Scotch Whiskey	Aged Scotch Whiskey
		Peach Schnapps	Cognac
		Baileys Irish Cream	Frangelico
Mixers	Ginger Ale	Club Soda	Bitters
	Cola	Coffee	Absinthe
	Orange Juice	Pineapple Juice	Pomegranate Juice
	Tomato Juice	Grapefruit Juice	Daiquiri Mix
	Cranberry Juice	Margarita Mix	
Other Drinks		Craft Beer	Craft Soda
Garnishes	Lemons	Limes	Mint
	Cherries	Salt	Umbrellas
	Fruits and Berries	Sugar	Olives
		Tabasco Sauce	
Equipment	Highball Glasses	Blender	
	Shaker or Stirrers	Strainer	

SAMPLE DRINKS LIST

Ginger Beer
(page 226)

Cafe Sua Da
(page 229)

Mudslides
(page 233)

Bourbon and Coke

Nonalcoholic Flavored
Iced Teas

Hot Pink Kisses Champagne
(page 222)

Daiquiris

Raspberry Mojitos
(page 225)

Sangria
(page 221)

Cordials and Liqueurs

Lemonade

Collect Supplies

Two Weeks Before the Party

Once you have selected your theme, food, and cocktails and have a good idea of who will be attending, you can begin collecting supplies. Start looking around for supplies and decorations that will match your theme. You will need to purchase basic supplies such as cocktail napkins, small plates, tablecloths, toothpicks, and extra wastebaskets. For a classier affair, you should always use cloth table linen, which will provide an extra-special touch. While you are shopping for these items, look for inexpensive store-bought decorations. This is also the time to begin stocking your bar.

Pick the Music

One Week Before the Party

The music you choose to play will help set the tone of the party. If you plan a sophisticated cocktail party, then jazz, easy listening, and classical music are good choices. If you have a themed party in mind, choose music that matches the theme. For example, for a Tropical Island Party, select some calypso or reggae music; for a 1970s Party, choose popular music from that decade; for a Southern Nights Party, choose music with a Southern theme, such as Harry Connick, Jr. or B. B. King. Play the music at a volume level that allows it to provide background ambience without overwhelming the conversation. If you don't have a large music collection, you may need to borrow from a friend's playlist.

Make the Food

The Day Before the Party

You should plan to make the more complicated treats, such as cooked meatballs, cookies, or lettuce cups, the day before your party. Present your appetizers in style. Consider unusual containers and unexpected garnishes to disguise the food's humble origins. A bag of chips and jar of salsa taste better if they are served in hand painted ceramic bowls. For some extra flair, add a parsley sprig to a bowl of bean dip or a put some lettuce leaves under a plate of shrimp skewers.

Try to keep things simple. The classic bread and cheese plate requires no cooking and little preparation, yet looks gourmet on a rustic bamboo cheese board or on a simple yet classy ceramic dish. Offer a variety of cheeses with lightly toasted, crusty French bread; rather than cutting slices, just set out a bread knife. Provide small jars of different mustards for an added treat. As a break from the standard stick-to-your-ribs fare, consider offering some fruit. There is no need to bother with an elaborate fruit salad; just display a couple bowls of bite-size fruit, such as strawberries or grapes, in decorative arrangements. Sausages and cured meats are perfect for a heartier snack. Just buy a few varieties of sausages at a gourmet shop or supermarket. If you have time, grill or broil the sausages before cutting them up to enhance their flavor. Select a few slices of cured meats and serve them with the same mustard you put out for the bread and cheese.

Last-Minute Preparations

The Day of the Party

The morning of your party, prepare the last of your food and refrigerate it so that it will be ready to pull out just before your guests arrive. Spread your tablecloths and arrange the furniture to facilitate conversation. Set out a few extra wastebaskets so that your house does not become littered with empty cups and used plates. If you are hosting your party in a rented space, begin transporting your food and supplies as early as possible so that the final hours before your party can be spent on any emergencies that arise.

A couple of hours before your party, run through your bar items one last time to ensure you have all your ingredients. You may need to run to the liquor or grocery store for last-minute purchases. If you have enlisted a bartender (who could be a friend) or any other help, these people should arrive at least one hour before your party begins. This will give them time to become familiar with their surroundings. During the party you may need to refill the hors d'oeuvres. You can also ask another helper to be in charge of this aspect of your event. Being well prepared will ease your stress when the guests begin to arrive.

- four -

Engagement Celebration

Engagement parties are customarily traditional affairs. This example details a formal engagement party. However, these days people use a wide variety of themes for their engagement celebrations. Do not feel constrained by stuffy customs; let your imagination run free and be creative within your practical limits.

This chapter provides a framework around which you can develop an engagement party that suits your honorees. The larger and more elaborate the party, the more planning, preparation, and delegation will be required. Smaller, more intimate parties will require less work, but limit the number of guests you can invite.

Pick a Style or Theme

Eight to Ten Weeks Before the Party

Engagement parties are an enjoyable way to formally announce an engagement and celebrate a union not only between two people but between two families. This party is the time for cultivating the relationships among future wedding guests, so planning it is a large responsibility. When picking a style or theme (if you choose to have a theme), it is important to take into account the personalities of both families. If both families are fairly casual and laid-back, it may not make sense to have a formal, black-tie affair. If both families share a tradition or nationality, a themed party—such as a beach theme for seafaring families or a traditional Old World theme if both families have roots in the same country—may be in order.

Stylist: Carolyn Chen, The Special Day

Traditions and Etiquette

An engagement party is an important initiation to the succession of ceremonies surrounding a wedding. However, if you know the rules—and keep a healthy perspective about breaking them—your focus will be less on ceremony and more on fun. The key is to communicate with everyone involved to determine which rules are important, and which rules should be broken. Here are some traditional rules and their exceptions:

DRESSING THE PART

Rule	Exception
The bride's parents sponsor an engagement party.	The couple themselves or the groom's parents may want to be more involved.
The father of the bride gives the first toast.	If he is not present, consider asking the father of the groom or a favorite uncle of the bride.
No one who is not invited to the wedding should be invited to the engagement party.	If the wedding is an intimate one, the couple may choose to make the engagement party the main celebration with friends who will not attend the wedding.
Guests are not expected to bring gifts.	Guests may decide to bring gifts anyway. Be discreet about stashing them and open them at a later time.

Plan the Party

Eight Weeks Before the Party

It is a good idea to hold the engagement party at least one month—or up to three months—after the couple has actually become engaged. This will give them a chance to get used to their new status and relax before all the madness of wedding planning begins. This party should not add to their stress, but rather should give them a chance to relax and celebrate with those they care about. You will need to do three main things when planning the party: consider the guest list, decide on a time, and pick a location.

Engagement parties are usually more intimate and casual than the actual wedding, although the bride and groom should be allowed to invite whomever they want. If the wedding will be very small, or at a great expense to the couple's friends, then it makes sense to have a larger guest list at the engagement party. However, the general rule is that everyone who is invited to the engagement party should ultimately be invited to the wedding. If the couple is planning a small wedding and want the engagement party to be a substitute celebration for many guests, be sure to let them know in advance so they do not feel shunned. If the couple is worried that their friends will think they are having a big bash solely to gather gifts, include a nice note in the invitation that requests no presents.

Engagement parties can be held during the day or at night, depending on your budget. Daytime parties are generally less expensive. Typical starting times are 12:00 or 1:00 p.m. for a lunch party, and 5:00 or 6:00 p.m. for a dinner party. If you are planning a less formal affair and want to serve finger food, you should start your party at either 2:00 or 3:00 p.m. for an afternoon party, or at 7:00 or 8:00 p.m. for an evening party.

Depending on the vibe you want and how many people you plan to invite, the site of the engagement party can vary. A beach, restaurant, boat, garden, vineyard, park, or home are all appropriate locations. Consider what type of wedding is planned, and hold the engagement party in a complementary setting for balance and variety. For example, if the couple is having a beach wedding, host a cocktail affair at a restaurant or on a dinner cruise rather than on a beach. If they are having a traditional church wedding, consider a garden or park for the engagement party.

Send the Invitations

Six Weeks Before the Party

For formal engagement parties, invitations should be printed on nice cards and embossed if possible. When choosing an invitation design, look for something that matches the theme of the party. This can be as simple as using a brightly colored card stock for a beach setting, or using a card with a flower border if you are holding the party in a garden. Gold or silver ink is always a nice touch.

Be sure to include an RSVP card with a self-addressed, stamped envelope and the deadline by which it should be returned. You can request that people RSVP by e-mail if you prefer, just be sure to print your e-mail address on the card. Remember that older family members and guests may prefer to RSVP by mail, and consider including an RSVP card for them even if you expect all other guests to RSVP by e-mail. You should request that people RSVP at least two weeks before your party. The number of guests will be one of the key components to planning the rest of the party. Avoid electronic invitations unless you are having an informal gathering.

AN ELEGANT ENGAGEMENT PARTY INVITATION

Please join us for brunch to celebrate
the upcoming marriage of

Trinh & Carlo

Saturday, November 5
Two Thousand Eleven
Eleven o'clock in the morning

Celebration Hotel
9400 Inspired Boulevard
Celbration City, California 91028

RSVP by September 30
To e-mail@gmail.com

Choose the Food and Drinks

Five Weeks Before the Party

The food and drinks you serve at the engagement party will largely depend on what kind of party you have. If you are having a beach party, choose some tropical dishes. If you have a garden party, salads and lighter fare are in order. For an Old World theme, pick some traditional dishes from the couple's homeland. If you are having a catered affair, or are holding your party at a restaurant for a large group of people, plated dinners served by waiters are best to keep traffic and crowding to a minimum. Remember, you should plan to hire caterers about six weeks before the party. For smaller groups and more casual parties, buffets work well. If you are on a tight budget, consider serving cocktails and coffee along with simple hors d'oeuvres and desserts. This option tends to work better if the party is held at night. For couples with a more casual style, it might be fun to have a potluck or a barbecue.

Many families like to enjoy beer, wine, and other spirits at their celebrations. Engagement parties are no different. Along with the food, you may want to provide a simple do-it-yourself bar arrangement, or hire a bartender (see the advice on stocking a bar on page 38 for more information). Some formal engagement parties include a full open bar or a wine bar. If the party is a casual beach affair, beer is appropriate. For an elegant garden party, offer some chilled chardonnay. No matter what the theme or food choices are, champagne is a must.

Decide on Activities

Four Weeks Before the Party

When it comes to the activities at the party, you must once again consider your style and theme. If the party will be made up of a small group, sometimes icebreakers and games can help set a fun and playful mood. If you are hosting a formal gathering, the only activity needed may be a small dance floor. For an informal beach or pool party, you might consider some more active games such as sand darts or limbo. If you are renting a restaurant with a bar area, you may have access to billiards.

It is often a good idea to include some casual trivia games, with the questions focused on the soon to be married couple. If you do want to have games and dancing, consider putting a responsible friend in charge, so that the props (if necessary) are planned and the sound system and playlist are under control. This way, you can attend to your guests, the atmosphere of the event, and any last-minute details. With one less thing to worry about, you can enjoy the evening just as much as your guests do.

Toasts are another common activity at engagement parties. Tradition dictates that the father of the bride should be the first to toast the couple. He is often followed by the groom and one or two others, although this is not mandatory. You should discuss the toasts ahead of time to ensure that the potential speakers are comfortable giving a toast. Remember to be flexible at the party and play it by ear—if anyone else wants to make a toast, they can always do so.

COMMON ENGAGEMENT PARTY ACTIVITIES

Commitment ceremony or engagement certificate signing

Roast of the engaged couple

Exchange of token gifts (such as coins or a handkerchief)

Presentation of guest favors

Announcement of attendants

Guests sign a book or poster and offer advice

Select the Party Favors

Three Weeks Before the Party

There is no better way to say thank you to your guests than to give them a party favor. This is also a great way for them to remember the special occasion. Favors do not have to be expensive, and there are many options available. You can also be creative with handmade items to save money. Just remember to select favors that match the theme and are fun.

PARTY FAVOR IDEAS

Bottle stoppers

Coasters

Cookie cutters

Homemade desserts

Miniature champagne bottles

Monogrammed candles

Picture frames

Collect Supplies

Two Weeks Before the Party

Take some time to collect the supplies you will need for the party. If you are having a beach or pool party, you may need to borrow some tables and chairs from friends or rent them from a party supply store. You should also start collecting and buying things like the tablecloths, plates, napkins, and cups. If you are having a formal party, you may have a caterer handling most of these supplies. In this case, you will only need to collect accent items such as table centerpieces, party favors, and name cards. If you are planning your own formal party, be sure to have all the linens, glassware, chinaware, and silverware planned at least two weeks in advance.

Prepare the Food

One Week Before the Party

A formal, sit-down dinner will most likely require a caterer—or at least a few helping hands—when it comes to preparing and serving the food. If you are having a small party and want to prepare the food yourself, you will need to do most preparation ahead of time. Try to select recipes that can be made ahead of time to a certain point, then refrigerated and heated in the oven at the time of the party. If you are making your own food for a buffet, consider dishes that are easy to fit in chafing dishes and will stay warm.

Make Ahead Sit-Down Dinner Dishes

- Turkey and Vegetable Lasagna (page 185)
- Pork Tenderloin (page 187)
- Beef Bourguignon
- Green Bean Amandine
- Herb-Roasted New Potatoes (page 196)

Buffet Dishes

- Shrimp Skewers (page 171)
- Mini Barbeque Turkey Sliders (page 181)
- Asian-Inspired Meatballs (page 176)
- Manicotti
- Carrot and Cabbage Coleslaw

Last-Minute Preparations

Three Days Before—and Up to the Morning of—the Party

If you are having your event catered, be sure to touch base with the caterer at least three days before your party to make sure all the details are secure. Will they be providing tablecloths for all the tables? Are there enough dishes for all the guests? Is the bar stocked with everything you requested?

If you have hired entertainment, this is a good time to contact the performers as well to confirm that they are still on schedule. Three days before is a good time to double-check these elements to ensure there are no surprises. If you are setting up for the party yourself, be sure to have everything you need at the location, set up, and ready to go at least one hour before your guests are scheduled to arrive. This will give you time to make any last-minute adjustments, and allows you to be totally confident that everything is in place when the party starts.

five

Graduation Party

The days of pep rallies, class trips, team practices, and school plays are coming to an end for your child. Graduation is an exciting time of transition. There is some sadness about saying good-bye to the past, but this feeling is mixed with excitement for the future. Keep all of these feelings in mind as you plan the party for this milestone occasion. Involve your graduate in the planning process. Make it a memorable event that initiates their next stage of life.

Pick a Style or Theme

Eight to Ten Weeks Before the Party

It is always better to have a theme for this kind of party. Graduation alone is enough cause for celebration, but you will need something more to pull your party together. Adding elements that relate to the interests of the graduate will make the party more fun, and it will be easier for you to decorate.

Graduation parties usually occur during the summertime. You can often take advantage of the time of year to host an outdoor party. You could have the party in your own backyard pool or rent out the community pool. If you live near the ocean, you can have a causal beach party. Keep the decorations colorful, fun, and simple. If your recent graduate already knows his or her path for the future, model the theme around their major or vocational choice. For college graduations, you might consider hosting a more sophisticated party such as a riverboat dinner cruise. Decorations can relate to the recent graduate's chosen career path.

Stylist: Sonia Sharma, Sonia Sharma Events

Plan the Party

Eight Weeks Before the Party

As with all of the parties, you will need to determine the time and location of your party, but first you will need to decide how large of a party you want to have and how many guests you will invite. Should the party be for only family members? Will classmates be invited? Are you inviting the entire neighborhood? Since this is a party for your graduate, ask him or her for input. Some kids may want to help and some may not. If your graduate wants to be involved, have him or her make a list of friends to invite. Be prepared for this list to change many times.

Once you have the guest list established you will need to decide when to hold the party. Setting the date and time for a graduation party can be harder than you anticipate. If you want to host the party immediately after the graduation ceremony, you will probably find yourself competing with other parties. This is fine, but keep in mind that your graduate's friends may be traveling from party to party without staying long in one place. This will make your party more of an open house type of event. You should try to coordinate the party so that the most people can attend.

Before you finalize your plans, have your graduate talk to their friends to find out if you are hosting the only party in town that night, or if yours will be one stop among many. Remember that your graduate might want to attend other friends' parties as well. Be flexible in selecting a date. Write down a few options and start calling the people you would like to invite. Narrow down your choices until you have selected the date that suits the most people.

When you have the guest list, date, and time selected, you will need to decide where the party will be held. Since graduations are usually held in the late spring or early summer, it is tempting to plan an outdoor party. If you choose an outdoor location for your party such as a park or garden, be prepared for bad weather. Plan to use a tent or alternative location if it rains. Fun indoor options for this type of party include a hall, movie theater, or bowling alley. If you have access to a lake house or mountain cabin, these are good locations for smaller parties. Whatever location you choose, you should make the reservation for the event as early as you can. Now is the time to book the caterer, too. If you plan to host the party at your home, go ahead and jot down things you will need to rent, such as tables, chairs, or a tent.

Send the Invitations

Six Weeks Before the Party

It is important to start your party off on the right note, and this requires that you send out a great invitation. If you are having a pool party, let your guests know the theme of your party instantly with a pool-themed invitation. Your graduate has earned it, so treat them to a great invitation that matches their style and interests. You can also send traditional, engraved invitations, or select something more whimsical, such as an invitation that looks like a diploma. There are templates available online, or you can make your own. Order the thank-you notes at the same time you order the invitations. This way your graduate will be able to write and send these out immediately after the party.

GRADUATION POOL PARTY INVITATION

Choose the Food and Drinks

Five Weeks Before the Party

The food at the party should reflect the tastes of the guest of honor. Ask your graduate what he or she would like to have served. Even if the food they select is unsophisticated—like pizza, hotdogs, or nachos—be sure to include these options on the menu. You can always add a more grown-up twist to the menu to celebrate the milestone. Provide a fancy flatbread pizza, or select specialty sausages instead of hotdogs. If you are using a caterer, meet with them about two months before the party to plan the menu, which should match the theme and style of the party. If you plan to cook the food yourself, you should make a very detailed timetable for your party including when you will shop and cook (see page 236 for a sample preparation chart). An easy alternative to formal catering is to order pizzas, or hero or hoagie sandwiches, for the group. Whatever route you choose, accept offers of assistance from friends and relatives for the cooking, serving, and cleanup.

If you have a pool party or other outdoor party in the early summer, it is important to have plenty of water on hand. Your guests will be tired from all the partying, and the sun dehydrates people quickly. Provide bottled water for easy accessibility to water. You can decorate the drinks by using straws with graduation hats or school banners. Other drinks to consider serving include sodas, iced tea, or fruit punch. Be sure to have a few recycle bins on hand for all the empty plastic bottles.

Plan Keepsake Activities

Three Weeks Before the Party

Think about ways to make the party memorable for your graduate. Written reminiscences are a great way for your graduate to reflect on his or her school years. Consider some various activities for creating memorable keepsakes. You want to ensure your graduate will look back on the day with fond memories, but keep it simple. Don't plan too many activities, but consider these ideas to get you started:

- Memory Board

  Choose a couple dozen photos of your graduate and friends and glue or tape them to two or three white foam boards. Make a permanent marker available so that guests can sign them like yearbooks. Have guests write down what they think will become of the graduate so he or she can look back on it in ten years for a laugh.

- Scrapbook

  Choose a couple dozen photos and paste them into a scrapbook. Provide different colored pens that guests can use to contribute a memory to the book.

- Time Capsule

  On the invitation, ask fellow graduates to bring something that relates to their experience in school. Place these items in a box and give it to your graduate for safe keeping until their ten-year reunion.

- Memory Notes

  Create a note box with a slot or hole in the top for each fellow graduate guest. Old tissue boxes work well for this. Set out stacks of note cards and pens. Instruct the graduates to write down their memories of each other on the cards and place them in the respective friend's box.

Delegating Tips

This is your child's graduation party, and you need to enjoy the event as well. Do not take all of the responsibilities on yourself. Whether you enlist the assistance of a sibling, spouse, or hired helper, learn to delegate.

- Bathrooms

  If you are hosting the party in your home, you might consider renting a couple of portable toilets, depending on the size of the party. Otherwise, ask a friend or relative to periodically check your bathrooms to make sure there are enough supplies.

- Food and Drinks

  If you do not use a caterer, ask a friend to help you prepare the food ahead of time. Put someone in charge of keeping the buffet tables and drinks stocked.

- Cleaning Up

  Be sure to have enough trash cans available to ensure minimal litter. Ask a couple of people to be responsible for clearing overflowing tables.

- Video Taping

  Place the video camera on a tripod and just let it roll.

Collect the Supplies

Two Weeks Before the Party

The best option is to use biodegradable, disposable plates, napkins, and utensils at a graduation party. A good rule of thumb is to buy enough of these supplies for twice the number of guests you expect. White Chinet plates are fine, but you can kick the decorations up a notch by using graduation-themed paper goods. Even if you just use themed napkins and dessert plates, this detail makes a big statement. Consider the interests and planned major of the graduate when collecting your supplies. You can also opt to customize the decorations by using the school colors of the school the graduate attended or plans to attend.

If you are hosting the party outside at your home, consider the number of tables and chairs you will need. Your guests will need a place to sit down and relax. You may need to borrow or rent extra lawn furniture. You will also want to have a couple long folding tables for the buffet. Make sure you have tablecloths for the buffet tables.

Make the Food

The Day Before the Party

If you decide to make the food yourself, try to make as much of the food as you can ahead of time. Try to select food that can be prepared up to a certain point and then baked on the day of the party. If pizza is on the menu and you choose to make your own, assemble the pizzas ahead of time, wrap them in foil, and freeze them until the day of the party. If you plan to have a vegetable tray, you can cut up the vegetables two or three days in advance and store them in the refrigerator in ziplock bags with a piece of wet paper towel inside to keep them crisp. If you are grilling hotdogs and hamburgers, clean the grill ahead of time and make sure your propane tank is full. You can make hamburger patties in advance and freeze them until the day of the party, or save even more time by buying ground beef patties at the store.

Last-Minute Preparations

The Day of the Party

If you are using a caterer, call the morning of the party to confirm that everything will take place on schedule. Set up all the tables and chairs early, and make sure you have enough table coverings. If you are hosting the party at another location, begin transferring your food and supplies to the party venue as early as possible. You will want to finish setting up at least an hour before your party in case you encounter any emergencies.

If you are grilling, double-check the grill to make sure it works. This is also when you should set up your keepsake activity, arrange balloons, and hang your themed decorations. All the nonperishable food items, like water, soft drinks, chips, and pretzels, should be on the buffet tables. Thirty minutes to an hour before your guests arrive (depending on how much cooking you have to do), begin cooking the food that you prepared ahead of time. This will give you plenty of time to relax and prepare yourself for the celebration of this momentous occasion.

six

Housewarming Party

A housewarming party is a time to show off your new—or newly renovated—home to friends. The move into a new home is one of the more exciting events in life. This occasion is definitely a time to break out some treats and celebrate. While a housewarming party is a good excuse to celebrate with friends, it is also a great way to meet people in your new community.

The wonderful thing about a housewarming party is that you do not need to wait until your home looks perfect, or even until everything is unpacked. People understand that it takes a long time to get settled, and they are too eager to see the new house to care whether you have hung the curtains yet. The good thing about housewarming parties is they can be informal and simple, which is a relief after the craziness of moving.

Plan the Party

Six Weeks Before the Party

Most parties take weeks to plan, but you have been preoccupied with moving or renovating, and have probably not had much time to plan. It is still best to set a date four to six weeks in advance. Your home's appearance will probably be less than perfect for months to come, but you want to ensure that you have enough time to organize and properly show off the new house. There is no need to spend a lot of time on a theme; this is a housewarming party. Throw a simple party and invite your regular crowd, but be sure to include some of the new neighbors to give yourself a chance to get to know them.

Stylist: Lucia Dinh Pador and Henny Vallee, Utterly Engaged magazine and D*LSH Design Studio

Decide what kind of party you want to throw, and who will be invited. Will the party be for adults only, or will it be an afternoon get-together for families? What time you will have the party? Remember that an afternoon get-together is more casual than an evening affair. If you have children, this can be a great way for your kids to meet other kids in the neighborhood. You can have a party with a definite start and end time, or you can throw an open house party, leaving people free to come and go all day as they are available.

Send the Invitations

Four Weeks Before the Party

Housewarming parties are usually casual events. Formal invitations are unnecessary. Make postcard invitations using a photo of the new house, and be sure the address is included in the invitation. Provide good directions to help your guests to find the home more easily. Consider dropping off the invitations for your new neighbors in person, which will give you a chance to introduce yourself ahead of time.

How to Make a Postcard Invitation

1. Select a photo of your house and print the image on your computer printer on 4x6-inch photo paper. You can also buy card stock at an office supply store.

2. Print the party details, making sure to include date, time, address, and driving directions on large stickers. Place these on the back of the photo on the left side (see the photo to the right).

3. Address the card on the other half of the blank side. There is no need to ask for RSVPs. Instead, let people know they can drop by between specific hours.

Choose the Food and Drinks

Two Weeks Before the Party

Whether you decided to have an afternoon event and serve light snacks or an evening affair with wine and hors d'oeuvres, be sure to keep things simple. Buy all the food you plan to serve—this is not the time to show off your culinary skills, unless you have the time and friends who are willing to lend a hand. The search for specialty food stores and bakeries will give you a good excuse to explore your new neighborhood. You can freeze most of the prepared food you buy.

When exploring the stores, keep a list of items you will need to buy fresh. Make a trip back to the market the day before or morning of your party. An afternoon party with tea, cookies, nuts, chips and dips, a cheese plate, and juice will not require much preparation. Your friends and neighbors will not expect too much fuss.

If you plan to host an evening reception and serve wine, you can ask people to bring over their own wine glasses. Conversation about the different glasses can serve as an icebreaker as people compare shapes and styles. This will also save you from washing dozens of glasses. For an evening party you probably want to serve more sophisticated snacks such as Asian-inspired meatballs (page 176), bacon-wrapped dates (page 155), or bruschetta (page 165). For an afternoon party, consider serving appetizer versions of breakfast foods to give the party a comfortable and homey atmosphere.

At a housewarming party, the house is the main event, and you should plan on giving tours. At an afternoon party or an all-day open house—with children in attendance and people coming and going—you will probably want to give tours yourself every twenty to thirty minutes. Have your significant other or a close friend act as host, answering the door, welcoming your guests, and making them comfortable until the next tour begins.

You can also designate a close friend or family member to act as a tour guide for you or provide your guests with a floor plan of your home for a self-guided tour. On the map, label each room with its name, purpose, and any interesting details you may want to show off. If you have made extensive renovations to your home, post "before" pictures outside each room that has been renovated. Your guests will love to see the magical transformation.

You should try to clean and tidy up all of the rooms you plan to show. If you don't mind a few boxes being visible, be sure to place them out of the way. If orderliness is one of your priorities, pick a room or two to store all the unpacked boxes, and only show the rooms that are neat and clean.

Collect the Supplies

One Week Before the Party

Since you have only recently moved into the house, the pressure is off when it comes to elaborate decorations. Do not worry about making a centerpiece, buying party favors, or organizing activities. Still, a housewarming party is your time to bask in compliments as your guests appreciate your catch. If you have time and are planning a large party, you may want to rent supplies like tables, chairs, and even dishes. If you are planning a smaller affair, it will probably be cheaper and more convenient to supply these items yourself.

Consider decorating using your own items such as books and throw pillows. These everyday items can look extra special when they act as accents in your otherwise minimally decorated house. Here are a few other easy things to consider doing to make the event special:

- Place a few scented candles in the rooms that are on the tour. This will provide a delicate aroma and soft mood lighting.
- If you prefer to use disposable plates and cutlery, be sure you have enough small wastebaskets out so that people can throw away their trash. This will ensure your new home is not cluttered with dirty dishes during the party.

- A guest book is a great way to remember everyone who came to your party. Place it by the front door, and encourage everyone to write little bits of wisdom in the book before they leave.
- Eclectic and punchy party music invites conversation and encourages relaxation. Keep the volume low, however, since you can not be sure of everyone's tastes.
- Make sure you have plenty of places for people to perch, lean, and sit. If you feel you do not own enough chairs, consider buying or borrowing some folding chairs for the party.

Final Preparations

Two Days Before the Party and the Day of the Party

You may have cleaned your home before you moved in and unpacked, but a quick cleanup before the party is still a good idea, and should be easy enough to do. Even if you have only recently placed all the furniture in its proper position after your move, you should rearrange the seating to create some conversation areas. Set out the food and drinks in a convenient place so that people can serve themselves. This will give you time to mingle with your guests and enjoy the party. If the weather is cold, clear out the front closet or foyer to provide extra room for your guests' coats and boots.

If you feel concerned because you have not decorated your home or are worried that your home does not feel lived in, fresh flowers are a great way to bring warmth and cheer into your new house. There is no need to spend a lot of money; one large bouquet and a few small ones will add a lot of punch with little fuss.

Arrange all the cups, cutlery, plates, and any other supplies you will need. If you plan to serve cold beverages, you can use ice buckets, or keep the drinks in the refrigerator until you are ready to serve them.

Place the food on the serving table just before the guests arrive. Remember, if you have food that should be served close to room temperature, such as certain cheese, take it out of the refrigerator an hour before serving. Set small bowls of delectable treats in different locations around the house. To make guests truly feel at home, be sure you never run out of food, drinks, or music.

Take a moment to breathe and enjoy your new space. If *you* feel calm and at ease in your new home, your guests will feel more comfortable too. Keep the atmosphere casual and welcoming, and remember to take a few minutes to relax and recuperate from your efforts.

seven

Outdoor Movie Night

There is something special about the combination of a classic movie and a warm summer evening. They just go together so darn well. Watching a movie in your own backyard is a great after dark, outdoor activity. Today's technology makes it easier than ever to create your own outdoor movie party. This type of party is perfect for family, friends, and neighbors, and it is simpler to arrange than you might think.

Plan the Party

Three Weeks Before the Party

A movie night is a casual event, so it does not require very much advance planning. As with other parties, though, you will need to consider a few things: who to invite, what time to begin, and what foods and drinks to serve. What you don't have to worry about is the entertainment: just pick a movie and go.

First, consider who you want to come to the movie night. If you have a large space to make use of, consider inviting your neighbors as well as family and friends. When choosing a movie for your event, consider the crowd that will be coming and select a movie that is suitable for all age groups at your party. If there will be young children in attendance, choose a classic, family-friendly film. If you are inviting older kids, consider a PG comedy or a classic coming-of-age drama. For an all-adult party, you might select a more sophisticated option such as a 1950s classic, a foreign film, or a romantic comedy. There are several online catalogs that are organized by genre. These are great resources when it comes to deciding on a movie to screen at your party.

Stylist: Linda Ly, Grand Soirées Event Design & Coordination

Next, pick a time. Since you will want to screen the movie after dark, your party's start time will likely need to be after 8:00 p.m. If young children are attending, consider whether you can start earlier to accommodate their bedtimes. If the party is for teenagers or adults, you can move the starting time back to 9:00 p.m. or even later depending on the length of the movie.

Send the Invitations

Two Weeks Before the Party

As with the other parties, your invitations should match the party's theme. Since a movie night is more casual than an engagement or graduation party, electronic invitations are perfectly acceptable. Whether you decide to mail or e-mail your invitations, be sure to decorate them appropriately. Make use of such embellishments as a filmstrip border, or images of projectors, cameras, or movie canisters.

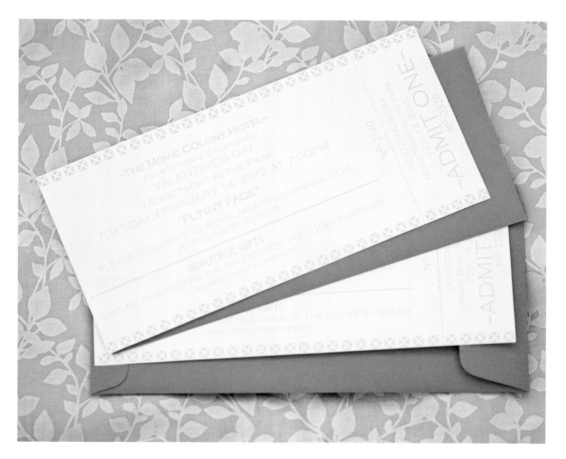

Collect the Equipment

One Week Before the Party

Since this party will be held outside after dark, you will not need to do much when it comes to decorations. You should provide some accent lighting to guide people to the house in case they need to use the bathroom. You can use a picnic tablecloth for the buffet table. If the food is away from an outdoor light, you will need to illuminate it with some candles or a battery- or gas-powered lantern.

Unlike some other parties, a movie night will require some technical skills. You can always enlist the help of a home-theater buff to prepare. You will need:

- A screen: Create your own movie screen using two strips of wood the length of a king-size bed. Tack an inexpensive king-size white bedsheet to the wood strips. Find a large outdoor area to mount the movie screen, making sure that the street and house lights will not interfere with the movie. Leave enough space so that your guests can sit far enough away to enjoy the show. You can also hang the sheet on the side of your house or garage. If it's not windy, you can even hang the sheet between two trees.
- Extension cords: since all of the electronic equipment will be outside, you will probably need a long, heavy-duty extension cord and a power strip.
- DVD player or computer and video projector: You will need to plug the DVD player or computer into the projector. There are plenty of places to buy a projector, or you can rent one just for the event. Ask around—you may even have a friend who owns a projector and will let you borrow it for the party.
- Speakers: You will need speakers that are powerful enough to broadcast outside so that all your guests can hear the movie. If you have a surround sound system, consider using wooden posts to mount your speakers around your seating area. There are also home theater systems complete with a projector and speakers available for rent.

Make Preparations

The Day of the Party

You will want to find the perfect spot to project your movie. This may be your backyard, patio, porch, or garage. You do not need to have a backyard to host a movie night—get creative with your space! Just make sure you select a location where you can control the amount of light at night. Avoid setting up your screen near a bright streetlight that could ruin the fun.

Accommodate everyone with comfortable seating. Place water-resistant sleeping bags and large cushions on the ground in front of the screen for younger kids. Lawn chair cushions work well for this purpose. Set up lawn chairs behind them for the older kids and adults. Families with young children may want to bring blankets in case the kids become sleepy. You do not have to provide seating for everyone yourself. Feel free to ask your guests to bring their own lawn chairs or blankets.

OUTDOOR MOVIE NIGHT TIPS

- Consider de-bugging the lawn before guests arrive, and provide bug spray for your guests. There are plenty of eco-friendly repellant options on the market. Place citronella candles around the viewing area to chase away any pests with wings.

- Use soft lights like candles or low-level outdoor lighting to create ambience. You want to keep the area dark enough to see the movie, but you also want to provide a little light for functional purposes.

- Remember to tell the neighbors you have a movie night planned. An outdoor event could potentially be disturbing to the homes around yours, so let your neighbors know of your plans ahead of time. You could even invite them to the fun!

- Check your equipment ahead of time. Some older movie projectors may have trouble with the sound, especially if you are playing some of the very old classics. You may want to test run the movie a night or two before the party.

Prepare the Food and Snacks

The Evening of the Party

Next you need to make popcorn—lots of it! The best popcorn is movie theater popcorn. If you happen to have a movie theater-style popcorn cart—or know someone who does—this would be perfect for your event. If not, the next best popcorn is homemade. Use a large, heavy-duty saucepan with vegetable oil to pop the kernels on your stovetop. For a large crowd, you will need to make your popcorn in batches, starting about an hour before the movie starts. Prepare at least one-quarter cup of unpopped popcorn per person. Serve the popcorn in movie theater–style boxes, which can be found at a party store, or in brown paper lunch bags. Make different flavors of popcorn to create a buffet. You may also want to make hotdogs and nachos. Look for paper hotdog trays or red plastic baskets to serve the hotdogs, and line them with parchment or wax paper. If you can't find plastic baskets or paper trays, paper plates will work.

Homemade root beer floats are another classic treat. Supplies for making homemade root beer can be found at home brewery supply stores. The easiest method for making root beer is to simply buy a mix to blend with seltzer.

CLASSIC MOVIE CANDY

These can be purchased the week before the party.

Milk Duds
(movie theater–size boxes)
Nonpareils
Twizzlers
Junior Mints

JuJu Fruit
M&M's
Ice cream bars
Soda pop served with straws

These kinds of snacks are fun treats for the little ones. For adults, they will bring back memories of good family times spent at the movies. Include your family in the party planning process. From hanging the backyard movie screen to making popcorn, group participation is what makes the backyard movie a deeply satisfying treat to enjoy, and such a great bonding experience.

eight

Overnight Bash

Everyone knows that a sleepover is about anything but sleep. These parties are a time for playing music, watching movies, and telling ghost stories. For most preteen girls, a sleepover is a chance to hang out all night with their best friends, do each other's hair, and talk about boys. Younger kids will probably want to camp outside, play flashlight tag at dusk, and tell ghost stories long into the night. Either way, sleep will be far from their minds, so be prepared to call it a night later than usual.

Plan the Party

Three Weeks Before the Party

A sleepover is a great opportunity to begin to teach your teen or preteen the basics of gracious hospitality. Of course, you will be the chief host of the party, but have your child perform some simple tasks like taking guests' coats when they arrive or passing out food. Learning how to put her guests at ease will give your child a feeling of pride and accomplishment. Begin talking about the responsibilities you expect of your child well in advance.

The first thing your child can help you with is the guest list. If this is your child's first time hosting a sleepover, keep the guest list short. Invite two or three friends so the party doesn't become overwhelming. If your child is a veteran of sleepovers, she might want to invite more guests. Five or six guests will be plenty, especially since the level of excitement at a sleepover tends to run high.

Stylist: Wilmarose Orlanes, Lovely Jubilee

Once you have the guest list set, determine good drop-off and pickup times. Since kids consider sharing meals to be a special treat, have the guests arrive in time for dinner. However, keep in mind that if they spend too much time together they can get on each other's nerves. To prevent this from happening before the night is through, don't have guests come too early. Planning the arrival time for half an hour before you plan to eat is a good rule of thumb. Likewise, arrange for a specific pickup time: an hour or two after breakfast is best. If you don't set a specific end time for the party, parents may drop in for their children at any time. It is best to keep the good-byes short and sweet, and a succession of sporadic good-byes can be chaotic for you and the guests.

Send the Invitations

Two Weeks Before the Party

Sending invitations early will create a buzz about your party. Ask for timely RSVPs— this will facilitate your planning process. As with other parties, ensure the invitations match the theme. Since sleepovers do eventually involve little heads hitting the pillow, consider a pillowcase-themed invitation.

Be sure to include a short list of things each child should bring, such as a toothbrush, toothpaste, sleeping bag, and pillow. If you are planning any special activities such as swimming or playing outdoors, let the parents know in the invitation that their child will need to bring a bathing suit, change of clothes, bug spray, flashlight, or other special items. For a campout sleepover, specify in the invitation whether or not the children will actually be spending the entire night outdoors. This way parents can prepare their children accordingly ahead of time.

Try to anticipate any special needs your child's guests may have. It is possible that your sleepover may be a child's first experience spending the night away from home without her parents. If you're not sure whether this will be a new experience for one of your guests, talk to the parents to confirm that their child will be comfortable for the night. You should also ask them if there is any medicine their child takes and get emergency contact numbers just in case.

Decide on Games and Activities

One Week Before the Party

Plan a few specific activities and remember to solicit your child's input. While kids will often manage to find their own entertainment, having several games and activities ready will help harness nervous energy and keep them from becoming mischievous and rowdy. Consider starting with some outdoor activities before it gets too dark, but have enough indoor ideas in mind to keep them occupied in case of bad weather. A word to the wise: if you award prizes such as DVDs, books, or MP3s, be sure you have enough for everyone to take something home, winners and losers alike. Preteens may seem mature enough to handle losing, but many are not. The last thing you want is to end up with pouty party guests.

OVERNIGHT BASH ACTIVITIES

When planning your activities, make sure there are enough supplies for everyone. If you plan on flashlight tag, for instance, ask your guests to bring their own flashlights and batteries. Be sure you have a few extra on hand just in case.

Outdoor Fun:

Capture the Flag

Flashlight Tag

Nighttime Hide and Seek

Indoor Activities:

Board Games
(Monopoly, Clue, Taboo, Cranium)

Card Games
(Hearts, Skip-Bo, Uno)

Charades

Movies

Scavenger Hunt

Have a plan to keep the kids occupied, going from one activity to the next until they wind down and are ready for bed. Organize your activities into blocks of time, such as:

5:00–5:30	Freeze tag
5:30–6:30	Two games of Capture the Flag
6:30–8:00	Pizza dinner
8:00–9:30	Flashlight tag or board games
9:30–11:00	Movie
11:00	Lights out

This will ensure the kids have enough to do and will stay out of trouble. It will also help you stay on track regarding bedtime.

Collect the Supplies

One Week Before the Party

Begin collecting the supplies you will need the week before the party. If you need extra flashlights, games, or pillows, now is the time to buy them. This way you won't be running around on the day of your party. Consider buying some party favors to give the guests as they leave. You may be able to find inexpensive mini flashlights, key chains, or bookmarks. Baseball cards work well for boys, and costume jewelry, headbands, bows, or pins for are great girls. Try to match the items in the favor bag to the party's theme. If you have an outdoor campout sleepover, send the campers home with all the supplies necessary to have fun outside. You could also choose to make something more sentimental for the favors, like a Keepsake Pillowcase (see sidebar on page 94).

Keepsake Pillowcase

During the party, pass out felt-tipped fabric pens and prewashed white pillowcases. Slip a piece of cardboard inside each case to keep the ink from seeping through to the other side. Have the kids embellish their cases with drawings and favorite slogans. They may even want to pass their cases around for everyone to autograph. With hand-decorated pillowcases to take home as favors, everyone can sleep on their memories for nights to come.

Choose the Food

A Few Days Before the Party

Stock up on food a day or two before the party. It will take a lot of food to feed a group of hungry preteens or teenagers. Buy some fun foods that everyone will enjoy, and have plenty of options. For dinner, provide food that is interactive for the guests, such as a taco bar, pizza bar, or pasta bar. Supply bowls of the various ingredients, and let each child prepare her own meal. This will please even the pickiest of eaters.

For a taco bar, offer ground beef, shredded lettuce, tomatoes, onions, and cheese. Be sure to provide plenty of taco shells—about five per teenager or four per preteen. For a pizza bar, offer different toppings such as pepperoni, ham, barbecued chicken, sausage, mushrooms, onions, pineapple, shredded cheese, and pizza sauce. Give each kid an individual-size pizza crust. You should buy at least two pizza crusts per child to be safe. For a pasta bar, make a huge pot of spaghetti. Let the kids fill a bowl with pasta and an assortment of other ingredients such as tomatoes, olives, onions, peppers, sausage, ham, cheese, and sauce. You may need to heat the contents of their bowls in a saucepan over medium heat for a couple of minutes to warm everything up.

Fondue is also a great option for a sleepover meal. You can start with cheese and provide fruit and chocolate for dessert. And don't forget to stock up on munchies! Buy some nuts and fruit, and also consider donuts, cookies, and chips for late-night snacking. For a backyard campout, s'mores are an awesome way to provide a snack that is also an entertaining activity.

Serve waffles or pancakes on the morning after the slumber party. Everyone likes to wake up to the smell of a sweet dessert for breakfast. Have a spread of traditional breakfast items ready for the kids when they wake up. Set up a waffle or pancake bar with a selection of toppings and syrups. Offer bacon, toast, and cereal as well, just in case someone doesn't care for waffles or pancakes, and provide juice and milk to drink. Be sure to take an inventory of your pantry the day before the party to make sure you have everything you need.

Prepare the Food

A Couple of Hours Before the Guests Arrive

Even though the kids won't be eating until later, it is a good idea to have all the food ready before the guests arrive. If you are planning a do-it-yourself food bar (taco, pizza, or pasta), begin chopping or shredding any ingredients you will need so you can bring them out just before dinner. If you are planning to order pizzas or sandwiches, call the restaurant early. Often they will be able to arrange for the food to be delivered at a certain time.

Prepare for Bedtime

A Couple of Hours Before Bedtime

If you are hosting a younger crowd, introduce a wind-down activity as bedtime draws near, such as watching a movie in their pajamas. Stay involved to make sure everything stays under control. You will want to ensure that the level of activity comes down a notch.

While the kids are occupied, prepare their sleeping area. Move furniture if necessary to clear an area for them to spread out their sleeping bags. Put out some guest towels and extra pillows in case anyone forgot their own. When the kids are ready for bed, have them arrange their bags in a starburst pattern with their heads toward the center. This way everyone is in the huddle, and no one gets left out on the edge.

It is important to establish a specific bedtime and to communicate this to both children and preteens. Some kids think that sleepovers mean they get to stay up all night. While you should expect that they'll talk and giggle for a while—that's the fun part—it is a good idea to have a set time for "lights out." For preteens, 11:00 p.m. is a reasonable bedtime. After you turn the lights out, tell them that they can knock on your door in the night if they need anything.

Make a Memorable Breakfast

8:00 to 8:30 a.m. the Morning After

Anticipate that the kids will sleep a little later than usual, but just in case there is an early riser in the group, try to get up early to prepare breakfast. If you plan on making a waffle or pancake breakfast, start by getting the ingredients ready. Set out toppings such as berries, whipped cream, chocolate chips, and nuts in bowls in a self-serve style. Try to have everything ready and waiting for them when the kids start trailing in the kitchen. If you start making bacon, the kids will likely wake up due to the pleasant aroma. Offer cereal and toast to those who don't like waffles or pancakes, but don't let yourself become a short-order cook for a group of picky eaters.

About a half hour before pickup time, tell the guests to start packing up their sleeping bags and other belongings. When it's time to say good-bye, have your child thank her guests for coming and pass out the party favors. Consider having one of your child's closest friends stay a little longer than the others. This way she will have some one-on-one time with her best buddy and is less likely to feel abandoned when everyone leaves. Keep this arrangement between you and the other child's parents to be sure the other guests don't feel left out.

- nine -

Tailgate Party

Atailgate party is usually organized before a sporting event. Normally held in an informal setting such as a parking lot, picnic area, or park, this event is called a tailgate party because the food is served on or near the tailgate of your truck or car. Tailgate parties involve little preparation when it comes to arranging the location. However, they can require quite a bit of planning when it comes to transporting everything you will need. If you are planning to host a tailgate party for friends or family, plan well in advance and pay close attention to details.

Pick a Theme

Six Weeks Before the Party

If you are planning a tailgate party at a college or professional sports arena, I have two words for you when it comes to decorating: team colors. Buy all your supplies—tablecloths, napkins, cups, streamers, balloons, drink cozies, folding chairs, radio, television, car (or maybe that's too much)—in the team colors.

The atmosphere of a tailgate party will vary depending on those who attend the party and those who plan the party. You can keep the festivities fun and low-key, or you can go all-out and have an extravaganza complete with a large screen television, comfortable seating area, and lavish food spread. It is not uncommon for tailgaters to compete over who has the best setup, to the point that some people will place full living room sets on the lawn or in the parking lot during a tailgate party. At a minimum, however, you will need camping chairs for your guests to sit on as they relax and enjoy the game.

Stylist: Lucia Dinh Pador and Henny Vallee, Utterly Engaged magazine and D*LSH Design Studio

Plan the Party

Five Weeks Before the Party

The first thing to decide is how big you want your party to be. Some tailgate parties—like the ones that feature a commercial meat smoker—involve spreads big enough for dozens of people. It is more common to plan a tailgate party for ten or fifteen people. Think about who you want to invite. Keep in mind that, given the nature of tailgating, people will be coming and going, and you will likely make a few new friends during the party.

Next you should consider the location. If you have some friends who are willing to help you set up, plan on taking the fewest number of vehicles as possible to the lot to save on gas, parking fees, and congestion. Arrange to meet somewhere before the game, and have everyone pile into a few vehicles. Don't be afraid to squeeze in tight.

If you have been tailgating at your home stadium for a number of years, you probably already have your favorite spot picked out, and that's great! But for those of you who travel to different stadiums, or are new to tailgating, take some time to learn about the venue. Keep in mind that most stadiums have restricted lots for season ticket holders. Find out which are the open lots and by what time you should arrive to get a spot. The alumni of some schools begin showing up days in advance to claim a good spot.

Decide early on which parking lot you plan to use. You may not know the exact location until game day, but you can put the parking lot and possibly the general area on the invitation. You should provide an easy way for your guests to locate you, so note on the invitation if you plan to put balloons or a flag on your vehicle. Many cars will be flying the team colors, so choose something distinctive, such as an inflatable mascot or a birdhouse (painted in the school colors, of course) on a pole.

BRING THE TAILGATE HOME

At this point, you may be thinking, *Couldn't this just be a cookout in my backyard?* In a sense, the answer to this question is yes. Such an arrangement may lack some of the energy and excitement that comes with thousands of fans tailgating together, but what it lacks in fervor it makes up for in comfort and ease. If you want to save money and still get a group together to watch the big game, this is a great alternative. Bring a couple of television sets out into the yard or use a radio to broadcast the game. You can even have people park their cars in the yard, if you have the room. Do all of the things you would normally do at an actual tailgate party, but within the comfort of home.

WHEN TO START YOUR PARTY

Game Start Time	Park By	Party Start Time
11:00 a.m.	7:00–7:30 a.m.	8:00–8:30 a.m.
12:00 p.m.	8:00–8:30 a.m.	9:00–9:30 a.m.
1:00 p.m.	9:00–9:30 a.m.	10:00–10:30 a.m.
2:00 p.m.	10:00–10:30 a.m.	11:00–11:30 a.m.
3:00 p.m.	11:00–11:30 a.m.	12:00–12:30 p.m.
7:00 p.m.	3:00–3:30 p.m.	4:00–4:30 p.m.
8:00 p.m.	4:00–4:30 p.m.	5:00–5:30 p.m.

Send the Invitations

Four Weeks Before the Party

You need to confirm the date and the time of the game before you invite guests to your tailgate party. Check the university's athletic department or team website for information about tailgating. You can also call the school's parking division (usually a division within the campus police department). If the game involves professional teams, call the stadium's front office to find out what time they allow people to begin parking near the stadium. Allow yourself at least an hour before your guests arrive to set up. If you plan to smoke or slow cook a pig or some ribs, you will probably need to start several hours before your guests arrive to ensure the food is ready before the game. A good tailgating party should last at least two hours, so factor this into the equation when giving your guests an arrival time.

Send the invitations at least four weeks before your party to allow your guests time to decide if they will attend and to purchase their tickets. Some games sell out faster than others, but four weeks is typically enough time for people to find tickets. Since you will need to know how many people are coming in order to buy the right amount of food, follow up with your friends or consider requesting an RSVP at least two weeks before the game. To make the invitations fun, find paper invitations in the shape of a football, or include a noisemaker in the envelope. Feel free to e-mail your invitations or use electronic invitations. Just be sure to ask people to confirm by e-mail or phone.

Fight On!
You are cordially invited to tailgate with us
Tennessee vs. Alabama
When: September 17, 2013
Where: Parking Lot 4 at the NE corner of Goal and Down.
We will be in the SE corner of the lot.
Look for the inflatable elephant in the sky.
RSVP to john@gmail.com or
(978) 888-2512 by September 1, 2013

Choose the Food and Drinks

Three Weeks Before the Party

Food is the most essential component of a successful tailgate party. A lot of people use tailgate parties as an excuse to fire up the grill and make everything from hotdogs and hamburgers to chili and ribs. You will want to choose food that can be either cooked on a transportable grill, or prepped ahead of time and easily transferred to a picnic area. You can sauté or grill onions and bell peppers ahead of time. Some other condiments you should consider include yellow mustard, Dijon mustard, ketchup, barbecue sauce, Worcestershire sauce, steak sauce, relish, sauerkraut, sweet peppers, jalapeños, blue cheese crumbles, Cheese Whiz, bacon bits, avocado, thyme, oregano, salt, and pepper. Don't forget the basics such as lettuce, tomato, pickles, and cheese. These options will give your guests plenty of choices as they create the Ultimate Hamburger (see page 182) or build their hotdog. Create a self-serve arrangement so that you will be able to enjoy the game with your guests!

Chili is a great tailgate party dish because it can be made a few days in advance and will warm you up on a chilly afternoon (see recipe on page 191). Transfer the chili into a large steel or iron pot and keep it warm on the back of your grill or on the side warmer if your grill has one. If you don't want to transport a grill to the parking lot, you can find small, propane-powered hot plates that will do the trick. Another hearty food option is pork shoulder. Like the chili, pork is something you can prepare well in advance. Both options allow you to feed a bunch of hungry fans, but still have a chance to enjoy the party.

In addition to the main course, be sure to provide plenty of snack food. Keep in mind that you should try offer food that people can eat with their hands or with as few utensils as possible. This will cut down on trash and clean-up factors, and allow people to eat without sitting at a table. Food such as sliced watermelon on sticks and grilled cheese triangles keep hands from getting too messy, and make cleanup simple.

MAKE YOUR TAILGATE A POTLUCK

Create a potluck list to accompany your invitation. This makes it easy for guests to sign up for items to contribute to the party. You might also want to list some non-food items like chairs and utensils. Make sure to send a reminder to each guest a few days before the event so that no one forgets what they signed up for!

Potluck Sign-Up
(for a party of six to eight people)

Check one and return to sender
___ Two packets of hotdogs
___ Two pounds of ground beef
___ Two packages of hotdog buns
___ Two packages of hamburger buns
___ Four bags of chips
___ Two 2-liter sodas
___ Four lawn chairs
___ Disposable plates, cups, napkins, and utensils

Drinks are a close second when it comes to items essential for tailgating. Beer is a common choice, but you can also add wine, martinis, and even whiskey to the mix. However, be sure to check the regulations of the stadium before you bring alcohol to the parking lot. Some places allow alcohol as long as it is inside plastic bottles, while others prohibit it completely. Either way, you should have a wide variety of beverages available in your cooler. If glass bottles are prohibited, you can bring cans of beer, plastic bottles of liquor, and boxes of wine. Be sure to include a couple bottle openers on your packing list just in case. Whether you're serving alcohol or not, be sure to offer plenty of bottled water so people stay hydrated. If you plan to serve alcoholic beverages, make sure each carload of guests has a designated driver. There is nothing fun about irresponsible drinking.

Decide on Entertainment

Two Weeks Before the Party

While the game will provide plenty of entertainment, it is sometimes fun to arrange a friendly wager on the outcome. You don't have to involve money; you can simply place bragging rights on the line. Use a poster board and magic marker to record everyone's predictions. To make it fun even for those who don't know much about the sport, you can break down the game into quarters. Bet on such things as the winner of each quarter, points scored in a quarter, the number of fumbles, number of interceptions, and so on. This way, people don't have to know as much about the teams to have fun betting. Choose music that will create an upbeat playlist to get everyone excited about the big game. Use a portable stereo and speakers so that you don't drain your car battery.

Keeping the Kids Entertained

Let's face it, no matter how exciting you may think the game is, younger children may not agree. It is probably best to find a babysitter for kids under ten, as it may be hard for young children to sit through an entire game. If you can't find a babysitter, find some activities to keep younger kids busy. Provide some small footballs for them to toss around. Pick up a few pom-poms from your local party supply store and have some of the older girls teach the kids some cheers so they can get in on the action. Bring a portable DVD player so they can watch a movie while the game is on.

Collect the Supplies

One Week Before the Party

Make a list of all the things you will need for the party. If you have asked people to bring items, now is the time to remind them of the things they signed up for. If you are providing everything yourself, keep in mind all the supplies you will need to consider:

- Folding chairs for seating
- Blankets to keep everyone comfortable and cozy
- Disposable utensils
- Folding table or two for serving food
- Serving dishes in the team colors, or tea towels or bandanas in the team colors that you can use to line baskets
- Pennants and other decorations
- Coolers and ice packs to keep drinks cold and to store food after the party
- Disposable plates, cups, napkins, and utensils
- Radio or portable television if you plan on watching the game from your tailgating spot

Final Preparations

The Day of the Party

The day of the game you will need to start getting ready at least three hours before the start of the tailgate party. For early morning games, you may want to pack your car with all of the nonperishable items the night before. Pack big items, such as the folding tables, chairs, and television, first. Pack your food items next. Wrap your casseroles and hot dishes with aluminum foil and cover them with newspaper or towels to keep them warm longer. Pack some baskets lined in your team colors from which to serve buns, rolls, cookies, and brownies. Dress in layers so you will be prepared for the ever-changing fall weather. Plan to leave early to claim a good parking spot. When you arrive, don't forget to display your pennants and flags to show your team support.

Once the game begins, be sure to pack up all the leftover food and drinks in your coolers. This way, instead of sitting in traffic after the game is over, you and your friends can relax and enjoy your leftovers for part two of your tailgate party!

GREEN TAILGATING TIP

Just because you choose to use disposable items doesn't mean you can't be eco-friendly. Look for bamboo plates and cutlery or for paper goods made from recycled paper. If you can't find eco-friendly, disposable paper goods, bring ceramic plates and silverware from home. Also, don't forget to bring plenty of trash bags to clean up after your the party.

ten

Oktoberfest

Autumn has arrived! The crisp days enhance all of the senses, especially our appetite. In the autumn we long for heartier food to warm us from the inside out. Potato soup, sausages, hot salads, dumplings, and beer—the refreshments of an Oktoberfest party—are just what the senses crave.

Historians say that Oktoberfest originated in 1810 as a wedding feast in Bavaria. This wedding reception turned into a huge festival, and proved so popular that it was repeated in the years to come. Think of this celebration as the arrival of the season for hearty eating. Today, Oktoberfest is a large, popular festival that features plenty of food, beer, music, and merrymaking. Despite the name, Oktoberfest is held during the last two weeks of September. In Munich, Germany, and in many other parts of the world, huge tents are set up in a meadow for the occasion, and the mayor kicks off the festivities by ceremoniously tapping the first keg of beer.

Pick a Style or Theme

Six Weeks Before the Party

Since you are celebrating a German festival the theme is predetermined, but you can decide how far you want to take it. You can choose to use traditional decor, or you can even go all out and dress the part. While it is not required that you dress up for your American Oktoberfest, you'll have a lot more fun if you do. Men should wear *lederhosen* (German for "leather trousers"), which are more like shorts. Women should wear *dirndls*, which are dresses with loose white blouses and a tight, often low-cut corset. If you plan to dress up for your party, consider letting your guests know that there will be prizes for the best costumes to encourage them to participate.

Stylist: Wilmarose Orlanes, Lovely Jubilee

Plan the Party

Five to Six Weeks Before the Party

A city-sponsored Oktoberfest can attract crowds of hundreds of people. Your party will likely be much smaller. Consider how many guests you plan to invite. Choose from friends, family, neighbors, and coworkers, the more the merrier.

An authentic Oktoberfest celebration is held outdoors during the last couple of weeks in September, leading up to the first Sunday in October. Consider hosting an outdoor party on the first weekend in October. If you have a big yard and don't mind people congregating on it, you may want to set up tents and tables. You could also use your driveway to give the party some more space. Another option is to turn your Oktoberfest into a neighborhood-friendly block party, if your neighbors are on board and you live on a quiet street. Check with the local municipality about blocking off part of the street, and be sure you are familiar with your town's policies on serving alcohol at such an event.

Send the Invitations

Four Weeks Before the Party

An Oktoberfest celebration is by no means a formal affair. For this casual party, an electronic invitation is acceptable. If you prefer to be more traditional, send paper invitations with the party details written in a gothic font. They will be appreciated and will create more excitement for your guests. Remember to include the date, time, and location. You can ask for regrets only. If you are familiar with your guests, feel free to request that they bring their own beer stein along with a few bottles of craft brew to provide for wide sampling of great beers.

OKTOBERFEST INVITATIONS

Oktoberfest at the Guevaras'

Bring a few bottles of your favorite craft
beer and celebrate Bavarian style!

When: October 10, 2013

Where: 1189 Pine Street

Dress the part. Come in your favorite
pair of lederhosen and dirndl.

Regrets only: tcguevara@gmail.com or (215) 855-6415

Choose the Food and Drinks

Three Weeks Before the Party

German food is the main feature of Oktoberfest, so it's important to provide a good selection of food with a distinctly German flavor. Some of our classic German favorites include:

- Leek and Potato Soup (page 179): Light and creamy, this soup makes an excellent first course.
- Soft Pretzels (page 177): Soft pretzels are easy to make at home, and your guests will be impressed to find you made these yourself. If you don't want to spare the time and effort, they are also available in the frozen food section at most grocery stores, and can be easily heated in the oven or microwave during the party. Serve these with a spicy yellow mustard.
- Bratwurst: A year-round favorite, this German sausage is best served grilled with a large side of sauerkraut.

- **Currywurst:** This is a grilled bratwurst served with a tomato sauce seasoned with hot chili powder and curry. It is a surprising treat with enough spice to take the chill out of the fall air.
- **Rotisserie Chicken:** Although this may seems like an American dish, rotisserie chicken is a big favorite at traditional Oktoberfest celebrations in Germany.
- **Potato Pancakes** (page 201): One of the tastiest German side dishes, potato pancakes are basically a mixture of shredded potatoes and onions mixed into patties and fried. They are especially good served with applesauce and sour cream.
- **Apple Strudel:** Nothing closes out a good Oktoberfest meal like apple strudel.
- **Black Forest Cake:** The Black Forest is the dense, dark forest where Hansel and Gretel got lost. This Bavarian chocolate dessert is as dark as the forest. Dare we say it's better than beer?

Guests will come to your celebration with a healthy appetite and an even healthier thirst, so make sure to stock up on a wide selection of beverages. Nothing goes better with your German sausages than a stein full of rich beer. In the early fall, it is easy to find various Oktoberfest-themed beers produced by both German and American breweries such as Samuel Adams Oktoberfest and Michelob Marzen. These specialty brews are fairly close to Marzenbier, a traditional German beer that was brewed in March and served later in the year. You may also want to pick up some German-brewed beer for a more authentic touch. Purchase a keg of a German lager, such as Löwenbräu, to accommodate most tastes, and offer a variety of darker German bottled beers for more discriminating palates.

Don't forget to have plenty of nonalcoholic beverages on hand, too, such as cider, birch beer, root beer, soda, and water. Your designated drivers will want to have something to put in their beer steins. For an extra-special touch, serve your drinks in authentic, one-liter beer steins.

BE A RESPONSIBLE OKTOBERFEST HOST

Because you will be serving alcohol, it is a good idea to ensure there are designated drivers so that anyone who enjoys Oktoberfest too much will make it safely home. Guests should drop their car keys in an appointed stein, which is then watched over by the "key master." Only those sober enough to drive can get their keys back at the end of the night.

Decide on Activities

Two to Three Weeks Before the Party

One of the main activities at an Oktoberfest is drinking beer; a close second is eating food. But, as at any outdoor party, it's always fun to make some games available for guests. If you decide to make the party kid-friendly, consider games like a ring toss, arrange for a couple of fun craft projects like pumpkin painting, and set up a tub of water so guests can bob for apples.

Collect the Supplies

Two Weeks Before the Party

Begin collecting supplies a couple weeks before the party. Keep in mind everything you will need for an outdoor party. It is best to have a tent large enough to accommodate your biergarten, food, and all your guests in case it rains or to provide shade. You can rent the tent from a party store. As an alternative, have several easy pop-up tents: one for the biergarten, one for the food, and a couple for eating areas. You may be able to borrow extra tents from friends. You will also need some long buffet tables and disposable plates, bowls, and cutlery. Instead of using folding chairs, look for benches, which will foster a feeling of community. Choose tablecloths in the Bavarian colors of cobalt blue and white, or in the German colors of black, red, and gold. Also keep an eye out for some inexpensive beer steins or large beer mugs.

For decorations, buy some Bavarian-colored blue and white streamers, or some German-colored red, gold, and black streamers, and hang them from the ceiling of the tent or from a pole in the yard. Collect some German memorabilia and ephemera such as flags, banners, advertisements, and crests to decorate the walls of the tent. You can also find pictures of beer steins online. Print and cut them out and hang them on the walls of the tent. Some of the last items to purchase are fresh flowers to decorate the tables. Lobelias and geraniums are traditional Oktoberfest flowers, but stalks of wheat can be a simple and unique alternative.

If you plan to have activities for youngsters, consider what supplies you will need. You can get an inexpensive plastic tub for apple bobbing, and there are a variety of sources for ring toss and bean bag games. Check your local toy store or search online at places like www.orientaltrading.com.

Make your list of items early so you don't have to scramble at the last minute. Consider calling a keg retailer to place your order in advance. The last thing you want is to find out there are no kegs of German beer left the day of your Oktoberfest.

German Freebies

Go to your local specialty market and ask the German beer distributors for any promotional freebies they may be able to offer you. If you are ordering a keg of beer, the distributors may be obliged to give you some glasses, banners, or posters. Remember, it doesn't cost anything to ask.

GERMAN TOASTS

When making a toast with those around you, make sure to clink the thick part of your mug or stein against theirs as you say "prost" (German for "cheers"). Remember that it's good manners to toast every person within arm's reach.

Prepare the Food

One Week Before the Party

Begin preparing the food one week before your party. You can make pretzels, cake, and strudel ahead of time. You can also prepare the potato pancake patties early, then fry them on the day of the party. Goulash and soup are good dishes to make ahead of time because it is easy to freeze and reheat them. If you have a meat dish, freeze it until the day before the party to ensure it will be fresh for your guests.

Set Up the Yard

The Day Before Your Party

It is important to have all the supplies at your house a day or two before your party. If you are renting a pole tent, have it set up the day before the party. Arrange your tables in rows to match the layout of beer halls.

Make some signs in German that you can use to tell guests where to find the beer ("biergarten") and appetizers ("happchen"). Officially welcome your guests to the party with an Oktoberfest sign in your front yard.

Decorate the tents to resemble the beer tents at Oktoberfest in Munich. Start by suspending a bouquet from the middle of the ceiling, and hang streamers radiating out from the center bouquet to the ceiling edges. This look costs little but looks authentic. Next, decorate the walls. Hang the German flags, Oktoberfest banners, and beer mug cutouts you have collected on the tent walls and on trees around the yard.

This is also the day to move any frozen food from the freezer to the refrigerator to thaw.

Final Preparations

The Morning of the Party

Get up early and finish your food preparation. Pick up your keg or kegs of beer. Arrange the food dishes on the buffet tables and put out the cups, napkins, and plates. Decorate your beer garden tables with a tablecloth, freshly cut flowers, and wheat, using large glass or ceramic beer mugs as vases. Finally, pour a large stein of brew and relax for a few moments before your guests arrive.

- eleven -

Bridal Shower

Expectations abound! Whether a baby is due or a wedding is right around the corner, showering your loved one with congratulations and gifts is an honor and delight. The following example focuses on a bridal shower, but remember that many of the same concepts can be applied to a baby shower as well.

Pick a Theme

Six Weeks Before the Party

Determine if your friend really wants to have a shower thrown in her honor. If this is a second marriage, the couple may choose to forgo the party. If your friend welcomes a shower, brainstorm theme ideas with her, keeping in mind the honoree's interests and tastes. If the shower is not going to be a surprise, ask the bride to be for her preferences. Be creative. Some ideas for themes include a formal tea theme, afternoon tea party, a kitchen-themed shower, an adventure theme, a sophisticated spa theme, or an elegant spring garden brunch. After you have selected a theme for your shower, choose decorations that will help to support your selection. The following example uses a Rustic Spring Brunch theme.

Rustic Spring Brunch decorations do not have to be over-the-top; you should aim for a simple, bright, and elegant display. If you are hosting the shower at home, you will need several large folding tables. Round tables are usually best. Consider using your best table linens and fine china, crystal, and silver, if you have enough. If not, disposable white tablecloths and clear plastic plates and glasses are perfectly acceptable for an outdoor party. Be sure to add some color, perhaps by using cloth

Stylist: Sonia Sharma, Sonia Sharma Events

napkins or placing wide ribbons down the center of the table. Decorate the tables with embroidered linen tablecloths and vintage plates along with your best silverware. Arrange colorful blooms such as roses, peonies, and snapdragons in a crystal vase to enhance the garden setting. Tie a few blooms together with a pretty ribbon, make a nice bow, and secure these bunches to the back of each chair to add to the decor.

Plan the Party

Five Weeks Before the Party

Consult with your friend to see what other showers are planned for the bride to be. Often multiple showers are given, and you don't want to duplicate themes or gifts. Ask the friends and family of the honoree if they'd like to chip in for the party. Typically the duties and cost of the shower are divided equally among all the hostesses (who are usually the maid of honor and the bridesmaids). Enlist the help of anyone who shows interest in planning the shower and has the time, or choose a cohost. A shower can be a daunting—and occasionally expensive—task to undertake alone.

If you are so fortunate as to have a cohost or multiple hostesses, consider the financial situation of all involved before making any plans. Given the average age of a bridesmaid is twenty-something, it is reasonable to ask for $30 to $50 per person. If you have four hostesses, your budget could be as much as $200. Every situation is different, so be sure to discuss this with the other hostesses and be flexible. Come to an agreement about how to divvy up costs and put the budget together. Your budget will likely determine your location, what food and drinks you will serve, the extent of you decorations, and how many people you invite. If funds are limited, hold a cozy shower at a hostess's home. If one of you has deeper pockets, perhaps consider holding the shower at a restaurant or even at a spa or resort.

Determining the location of the shower can prove tricky, and it depends on who will be attending. If yours is the only shower, then the bride's hometown is probably the best location for the shower. If your shower will be just for friends, then it might make more sense to choose the bride's college town or current city. Be sure to consult the bride for her preferences.

It is also essential that you consult the bride before setting a time and date for the shower. She is likely to be busy in the months leading up to the wedding, so check with her for open dates before you plan anything. Traditionally a bridal shower is held close to the wedding date, but some brides prefer to have it earlier in order to be free to handle all the last-minute details as the wedding date approaches. Most showers start anywhere between 11:00 a.m. to 3:00 p.m. Remember, every bride is different, so don't assume that this bride will have the same preferences and expectations as the bride from the last wedding you were in.

Traditionally, everyone who is invited to the bridal shower should also be invited to the wedding. If more than one shower is planned, try to avoid overlapping guest lists (although family members can certainly be invited to more than one shower, and the bride and groom's mothers should be invited to all of them). It is a lot to ask of a regular wedding guest to attend the wedding along with multiple showers, and to bring gifts to all of the above. However, if your shower is the only one the bride will have, then you will need to coordinate with the bride and groom (or with their mothers) to find out which family members or family friends need to be invited. Pick a date as far in advance as possible to accommodate out-of-town guests. If your guests are all local, shorter notice is fine. Decide whether to make the shower a girls-only event or a coed affair. While coed showers are very trendy, a traditional bride to be may want to go with a female-only fling.

Send the Invitations

Four Weeks Before the Party

Consider the theme of your party when selecting invitations. Choose attractive cards and decorate them with appropriate embellishments and fonts to match your theme. For a formal tea, use an elegant script font and a decorative floral border. For a sophisticated spa party, add some vellum paper, and, if your budget allows, include a sample size body lotion and perfume. For the Rustic Garden Brunch, use a script font, bright colors, and flower art.

Include registry information and request RSVPs a few weeks before the event. Confirm all reservations and RSVPs a week before the shower. Brunch invitations are traditionally somewhat formal, and often feature lighter colors and decorative accents such as ribbon. Try to match the shower invitations to the wedding invitations. You can either order the same pattern from the company the bride used, or choose an invitation featuring the same colors or a similar motif. Brunches usually begin between 10:00 and 11:00 a.m. Be sure to specify whether the party is a brunch, luncheon, or tea so the guests will know what to expect.

CREATE A BRUNCH INVITATION

Join us for brunch to celebrate the upcoming marriage of Margaret Jansen

When: Saturday, August 13, 2013 at 11:00 a.m.

Where: 2908 Overlook Drive, Raleigh, NC

Directions: From I-64 go south on Mall Road for 3 miles.
Take a left on Hillside Lane and continue for 2 miles.
Take a right on Overlook Drive. It is the sixth house on the right.

RSVP by July 30: call (412) 292-7322 or e-mail alisonsparty@gmail.com

The bride and groom are registered at Neiman Marcus, Nordstrom, and Macy's

Choose the Food

Three Weeks Before the Party

Next you should decide on the menu. If you are holding the shower at a restaurant, this will be easy. If you are hosting the shower in a home, decide whether you want to cater the affair, cook the food yourself, or go potluck. Keep in mind any special food preferences the bride or her guests may have, such as a vegetarian diet or food allergies. Brunches and luncheons are popular options for traditional bridal showers.

BRUNCH MENU

Here is a flavorful brunch menu that will put everyone in a celebratory mood:

Pomegranate Mimosas
(page 225)

Crab Quiche

Spring Greens with
Caramelized Walnuts and
Goat Cheese

Salmon or Tuna Tartar

Shrimp and
Cucumber Pasta
(page 195)

Chicken Wraps

Decide on Entertainment

Three Weeks Before the Party

Now is the time to plan the entertainment. There are a lot of fun games that are specific to bridal showers, but be sure the guest of honor will enjoy these games before you arrange to play them. The bride to be should be seated in style at the head of the table. If you wish to play shower games, choose some games that can be played sitting down so that your guests can linger over their food. Bridal Shower Bingo is a good option. Pass out bingo cards that have been filled with words that might be said during a wedding shower, such as dress, honeymoon, church, love, ring, and mother-in-law. Give each guest a marker to cross out a word when it's said. Whoever completes a line or blacks out a card first wins a small prize.

Fun Bridal Shower Games

- ### TP Wedding Dresses
  Break up into teams of three and have each team create a wedding dress out of toilet paper.

- ### Wedding Bells Mad Libs
  On pieces of cardstock, create cute but simple stories about some funny situations the bride and groom might find themselves in on their wedding day. Delete some adjectives, adverbs, nouns, or numbers and leave a blank space. Have guests brainstorm words to fit into each blank space in the story at the top of the card, and encourage them to get as creative as possible. Encourage guests with the funniest stories to read them out loud.

Another main event at the bridal shower is often the opening of gifts. Ask the bride if she would like to open the gifts in front of the guests, or if she would prefer to do this in private. The unwrapping of gifts can often be highly entertaining. Pick someone to write a list keeping track of who gave each gift if they are opened at the event so that the bride can easily write thank-you cards later.

To Gift or Not to Gift

If you receive an invitation to the bridal shower, you should definitely bring a gift, or send one even if you cannot attend the shower. This is in addition to the gift you will bring to the wedding itself. Consult the couple's wedding registry for ideas. Consider coordinating your bridal gift with your wedding gift. For example, present the bride to be with a coffee service at the shower, and then follow up with a coffeemaker at the wedding. Usually something within in the range of $20 to $75 is appropriate for a bridal shower gift

Collect the Supplies

Two Weeks Before the Party

Give yourself some time to collect all the supplies. As with other parties, you will need folding tables and tablecloths. You should inventory your china and silverware to make sure you have enough. If not, consider using clear plastic plates for certain foods. If you are having an outdoor brunch, make sure you have comfortable seating for people who are dressed up. Padded folding chairs work well, or you can rent wooden folding chairs for a nice touch.

Begin collecting your decorations. You can buy your ribbons and bows early, but purchase your flower arrangements a day or two before the party. Be sure to collect the supplies you will need for any games, and begin purchasing the nonperishable ingredients for your menu items.

You should also consider purchasing some small treats for bridal party favors. You can pick up some truffles and wrap them in decorative tissue tied with a ribbon. You might also consider peppermint bark or, for a spring garden theme, you could make some candied rose petals or give small bottles of rose water.

Make the Food

Three Days Before the Party

If you choose a potluck option, confirm with the people who signed up to bring something a few days before the party. If you are preparing the food yourself, you will need to pick up the perishable ingredients for the menu a few days before the party so you can begin making the food. To ease the burden, spread out the cooking over a few days. Make the foods that will keep first, and make the more perishable dishes, like a crab quiche or salmon tartar, the day of the party.

Last-Minute Preparations

The Day of the Party

You will need to solicit as much help as possible the morning of your party. If you can, have all the tables and chairs set up the day before the party. If this is not possible due to weather or space constraints, begin setting up the tables and chairs first thing in the morning. Tie the bows to the chairs, put the vases of flowers out on the tables, and hang pictures of the bride at various stages of her life. Try to have everything set up early so you will have time to put final touches on the food. If you are having the party at a restaurant, arrive as early as possible to hang streamers, ribbon and bow arrangements, and photos of the bride to decorate the room. Take a few moments before the guests arrive to reflect on the special day, and get ready for the fun.

twelve

Thanksgiving

Whether you're hosting Thanksgiving for the first time or the tenth time, making sure everything is organized and done in time can be daunting. At this time of year, we are inundated with idyllic visions of loving families gazing at a perfectly browned, moist turkey. Heaping bowls of side dishes are artfully arranged around the bird. The table has been set with the finest crystal and china that has been passed down from one generation to the next. The following tips will help you sit back and enjoy the family and friends this special meal involves without stressing about making your celebration fit anyone's image other than your own.

Pick a Tone

Ten Weeks Before Thanksgiving Day

It may seem obvious that you are getting together for Thanksgiving, but what is not obvious is exactly what kind of event you will plan. Thanksgiving Day could be a big, casual, kid-friendly gathering, or an intimate, elegant, grown-up meal. It could involve games, activities, and socializing all day long. It could mean making an event out of frying, roasting, or barbequing the turkey in the backyard. Or it could mean dressing up for a formal sit-down dinner and a reflection on the blessings of life. Picking the tone of the gathering will help you decide how many people to invite. The Thanksgiving spread detailed here is a formal adult dinner.

Stylist: Tracey Go, The Flower Tray

Plan the Party

Eight Weeks Before Thanksgiving Day

Thanksgiving is a time for celebrating with friends and family. If you have a large family and want to have an informal party, you may consider inviting a crowd. If you want to have a more elegant affair, it is best to keep the guest list short. You may want to take an informal survey of your family members and their ability to attend your Thanksgiving meal several months in advance to get an approximate head count before you start planning. Remember that your guests will need time to figure out their plans.

Unlike other parties, your Thanksgiving Day guests will need to know both when to arrive *and* when to expect to eat. Because Thanksgiving is traditionally a huge feast, guests will likely plan the rest of their meals for the day according to when they will be eating Thanksgiving dinner. It is usually best to have an early afternoon dinner to allow people time to develop an appetite, and the meal should be big enough to keep them satisfied throughout the evening.

Most Thanksgiving parties are hosted in the home. However, if you have too large of a crowd to accommodate in your house, you might consider another venue. Maybe another family member will open up her home and cohost the event with you. Some restaurants have private rooms for large gatherings. If you live in a planned community, a pool clubhouse can work well, as they usually have a large sitting area and a kitchen for food preparation. You may even consider a having outdoor party at a picnic area or pavilion. Be sure to reserve the space early to avoid any conflicts.

Send the Invitations

Six Weeks Before Thanksgiving Day

Make sure the tone of your invitation matches the formality of your event. Select a script font and delicate borders for an intimate, elegant dinner. A sans serif font with a horn of plenty image would work for a more festive party.

There are a few things you will need to include on the invitation for your Thanksgiving dinner. Because Thanksgiving is on a set day, it is more important to place the focus on the time of your party and the time you will eat. Be sure to include the address, even if you are hosting the party in your home. While your immediate family may know how to get to your house, some extended family members may have only a vague idea. Avoid confusion by including the exact address on your invitation.

Be sure to include two times on your invitation: the time to arrive and the time you plan to eat. You should plan on putting a few small snacks out while the final dinner preparations take place. But the most important thing for the guests to know is how to plan their other meals of the day around the main event of Thanksgiving dinner.

You will want to request that your guests RSVP so that you will know how much food to prepare and how large of a turkey to purchase. Formal invitations should have an RSVP card included. Casual and semiformal invitations can include RSVP information on the invitation. Be sure to include an RSVP date, contact information, and whether you want all guests to reply, or if you need regrets only.

If you plan on making your Thanksgiving meal a potluck, invite your guests to choose one specialty item to prepare and request that they include their choice in their RSVP so you can avoid duplicates. As the hostess, be prepared to make the turkey and any other items you think are necessary that guests do not offer to bring. Organizing a potluck can be a good way to make your guests feel as if they are contributing on a day that is about coming together to share with others. It will also take the strain of providing for a large group of people off your shoulders.

Pick the Decor

Five Weeks Before Thanksgiving Day

Thanksgiving dinner would not be complete without the decorative table setting we all associate with this classic American holiday. Whether you select an elegant theme or choose to go with a fun approach, the table decorations should make use of the colors of autumn leaves to capture the beauty of the season. Even if it is snowing where you live, use traditional fall colors such as red, orange, yellow, and brown to emulate the beauty of the autumn and provide your guests with a warm welcome.

For an elegant party, look for some silk garlands at a local craft store and pick one that uses fall colors. The same stores should have fake cranberries that you can put in clear vases of water to accent your table. For some additional fun decorations you might buy little pumpkins and gourds, which you may want to paint. Look for some wheat stalks that can be used as accents and save them for following years. All of these items should be available at a craft store. Be sure to have some scented candles in autumn themes such as pumpkin spice or pine scent, and light them before your guests arrive. A cornucopia filled with harvest fruits and vegetables is a gorgeous addition to the table for any type of party.

THANKSGIVING MENUS FOR BEGINNERS AND EXPERTS

| Easy Menu
Keep it simple and classic | Advanced Menu
Add new twists to the traditional meal |
|---|---|
| Herb-Roasted Turkey
(page 196) | Deep-Fried Turkey or Grilled Turkey |
| Canned Gravy | Savory Mushroom Turkey Gravy |
| Bread and Celery Stuffing or Sausage Stuffing | Old-Fashioned Stuffing
(page 189) or Sausage, Apple, and Cranberry Stuffing |
| Home-Style Mashed Potatoes
(page 202) | Garlic Mashed Potatoes |
| Sweet Potato Casserole
(page 197) | Roasted Root Vegetables
(page 198) |
| Sautéed Green Beans
(page 198) | Shredded Brussels Sprouts |
| Canned Cranberry Sauce | Spicy Cranberry Chutney |
| Store-Bought Rolls | Fresh Herb Dinner Rolls |
| Pumpkin Pie
(page 218) | Pumpkin Cheesecake |
| Pecan Pie
(page 219) | Chocolate Pecan Pie |

Choose the Food

Four Weeks Before Thanksgiving Day

Dinner is the main event in most homes on the big day, and the menu deserves plenty of thought. When preparing your menu, be sure to include at least one favorite dish for each guest. To make things fun, plan at least one new dish each year. This way you and your guests can discover together how the dishes turn out when they are done.

Collect the Supplies

Three Weeks Before Thanksgiving Day

Make a shopping list early, and plan to beat the holiday rush. The stores begin putting out their Thanksgiving decorations early, so take advantage of this and begin collecting your decorations almost a month before the party. This may seem excessive, but it will free you up in the weeks before the big day to focus on cleaning the house and preparing the food, which is no small task.

Begin your grocery shopping a couple of weeks before Thanksgiving. Organize your grocery list by perishable and nonperishable items. Buy all of the nonperishable items, such as canned goods, stuffing, flour, sugar, herbs, spices, marshmallows, chocolate, and nuts—and even perishable items that will keep, like potatoes, garlic, celery, carrots, and a frozen turkey—a couple weeks out. You might also consider suggesting to any co-chefs that they keep an eye out for bargain deals on turkeys.

Grocery stores usually have sales in the weeks leading up to Thanksgiving, but if you wait too long, you will often end up paying a higher price, which could be particularly bad if you need a very large turkey. Keep in mind when you are shopping for a turkey that you will need at least one pound per person. If you are hosting fifteen people, buy a 15-pound bird. If you are hosting twenty-five people, get a 25-pound bird. If you are hosting more than twenty-five people, consider buying two smaller birds, or supplement the turkey with a ham. Buy all of your perishable items, such as eggs, cream, vegetables, sausage, and bacon, a week before the party.

Cooking Tips

- Overestimate the time required to prepare recipes. Don't forget about sitting time; for example, after you take the turkey out of the oven, it should sit for thirty minutes before carving. Other foods might similarly need time to cool or rest.
- Remember that cleanup time is required between each recipe unless you have cleanup assistants to help you.
- Don't forget your limitations in terms of kitchen appliances. If you have only one oven, you will have to prepare some items in advance to free up the oven for other items.

Prepare the Feast

Two Weeks Before Thanksgiving Day

The trickiest part of preparing a large holiday meal is timing the cooking. The key is to make as many items ahead of time as you can, and reheat them on Thanksgiving Day. Here is a schedule to help you organize the day with ease:

Ten to Fourteen Days Before Thanksgiving

- Make and freeze Sweet Potato Casserole (page 197), add the topping later
- Make and freeze Pumpkin Pie (page 218) and Pecan Pie (page 219)
- Freeze store-bought or homemade rolls

Three Days Before Thanksgiving

- Place turkey in the refrigerator to thaw (birds larger than twelve pounds will require two to three days to thaw)
- Make the cranberry sauce
- Bake the pecan bars and place them in an air-tight container or on a plate tightly covered with plastic wrap and store in a cool, dry place

The Day Before Thanksgiving

- Toast the almonds for the green beans and transfer to a lidded container
- Cook the bacon, if using, for the green beans; crumble and mix with the toasted almonds and store in the refrigerator
- Make the mashed potatoes and store in the refrigerator
- Make the stuffing and store in the refrigerator
- Prepare the Pumpkin Cream Pie and cover with plastic wrap or place in an airtight container and store in a cool, dry place
- Set the dining room table, including serving utensils and serving dishes for gravy, dinner rolls, and butter
- Decorate the table with the cornucopia, garlands, berries, and wheat stalks

The Night Before Thanksgiving

- Place Sweet Potato Casserole in the refrigerator to thaw
- Prepare the gravy and store in the refrigerator

Very Early Thanksgiving Morning

- Add pecan topping to Sweet Potato Casserole
- Remove the top oven rack, if necessary, and preheat oven to 325°F to roast the turkey; after cooking, remove from oven and let stand for thirty minutes before carving

An Hour Before Dinner

- Increase oven temperature to 350°F and replace oven rack to bake the mashed potatoes, stuffing, and Sweet Potato Casserole

Half an Hour Before Dinner

- Wrap the dinner rolls in foil and place in the warm oven to heat
- Warm the gravy in a saucepan over medium-low heat
- Prepare the green beans

Finishing Touches

- Transfer the gravy, rolls, and green beans into serving bowls
- Carve the turkey and arrange the meat on a warm platter

After Dinner

- Don't let the leftovers sit out for longer than two hours; wrap them up and put them in the refrigerator as soon as possible
- Make coffee, tea, and whipped cream for pies
- Soak the dirty dishes in warm water
- Serve the dessert with the coffee and tea and enjoy the end of your meal

Remember that Thanksgiving is a time to reflect on the good things in your life. While there is a lot of work and activity that goes into the preparation, keep in mind that the most important thing on Thanksgiving is to celebrate with friends and family. If something does not go as expected, let it be a learning experience. Go with the flow. Relax and enjoy the food, the company, and your blessings.

TURKEY COOKING CHART

The ready time includes thirty minutes of resting time before the turkey is carved to allow the juices to reincorporate. All times are approximations. The turkey is done when the thigh temperature has reached 180°F.

Turkey in Pounds	Cook Time Unstuffed	Cook Time Stuffed	Begin	Ready
8	2½ hours	3½ hours	10:00 a.m.	1:00 p.m.
10	3 hours	4 hours	9:00 a.m.	12:30 p.m.
14	4 hours	5 hours	8:30 a.m.	1:00 p.m.
18	5 hours	6 hours	8:30 a.m.	2:00 p.m.
22	6 hours	7 hours	8:30 a.m.	3:00 p.m.
24	6½ hours	7½ hours	8:00 a.m.	3:00 p.m.
28	8 hours	9 hours	5:30 a.m.	2:00 p.m.

thirteen

Winter Holiday

Winter holidays are important to many people and are always a fun time to celebrate with family and friends. Holiday parties vary widely. They can be anything from elegant soirées complete with linens, fancy centerpieces, and fine china, to casual affairs with lap eating, plastic plates, and fun drinks. This chapter combines both traditional and comfortable styles. There are many elements to throwing a successful holiday party, but it all comes down to a few basic steps: invite some friends over, enjoy some food and drinks, and celebrate good times together.

Pick a Theme

Eight Weeks Before the Party

When it comes to holiday parties, all you really need to do is decide how elaborate you want to make your decorations. Most people have a closet full of holiday decorations from years past. Take inventory of what you have. You might consider changing your style or adding new ornaments for the party. Decide this early on so you can have time to pick out the right adornments.

Plan the Party

Eight Weeks Before the Party

If you plan to provide a good amount of finger foods and desserts, you can hold your party around dinnertime and let the party food take the place of dinner. If you want

Stylist: Tracey Go, The Flower Tray

to have more drinks and less food, consider hosting an evening party around 7:00 or 8:00 p.m.—especially if the party is on a weekend night and your guests can relax and stay out late.

The type of party you want to throw and the amount of food you are willing to prepare will determine how many people you should invite. If you want to keep it cozy and go easy on the preparation, ten to twelve people is a good number for a holiday party. If you are ready to go all out, or choose to focus more on drinks than on food, you might invite twenty to thirty people. Remember, the attendees will create the atmosphere of the party, and having a group of ten to thirty people will encourage mingling. The following example, however, discusses an intimate party of six guests.

Send the Invitations

Six Weeks Before the Party

You can buy simple invitations at any local stationary store or online (see the resource section on page 241 for invitation sources and templates). Whether you decide to go with an elegant design or a fun, festive look, be sure to include the date and time of the party on the invitation. Also tell your guests what to expect regarding food and dress code. Be specific and give details. You can also add decorative images in the background or along the border. Be sure to let your guests know on the invitations whether or not you are planning a gift exchange.

Choose the Food and Drinks

Five Weeks Before the Party

When most of us think of the holidays, we think of eating large amounts of a wide selection of food. Providing a carving station with prime rib or ham at your party will ensure happy guests. Have some meat carved already to get things started, and see if an experienced friend will assist guests with carving.

Unless you are planning an intimate party with just a few couples, a sit-down dinner is not practical. For a casual meet and greet you will want to have plenty of snacks, appetizers, and hors d'oeuvres ready to go. A good rule of thumb is to prepare one menu item per three guests. If you invite fifteen people, prepare at least five different snacks, plus desserts.

Whether you plan to offer a more substantial menu or intend to stick to simple fare, put out a cheese platter with an assortment of cheeses, crackers, and fruit, and a bread tray with an assortment of spreads such as mustards, butters, and jams. A Crock-Pot filled with cocktail meatballs or chicken wings is a great way to expand your menu. To help your guests mingle, serve an assortment of holiday cookies, pastries, and mini desserts. This way your guests can select some sweets and walk around, rather than sit down to a huge slice of pie. Fill a bowl with mini candy canes and chocolate truffles as well.

Holidays are a time to celebrating with friends, drinks, food, festivities, and more drinks. Stocking a bar for your holiday party takes a little planning. You should plan to serve drinks that are festive and holiday-themed. The simplest way to serve holiday drinks is to follow a holiday color scheme.

If you celebrate Christmas, serve drinks that are red—such as vodka and cranberry juice, strawberry daiquiris, or red wine—and green—such as apple puckers, crème de menthe, or margaritas. If you celebrate Hanukkah, consider serving gelt martinis (made with potato vodka, Goldschlager cinnamon schnapps, and a drop of chocolate liqueur) or kosher wine. Hot apple cider, mulled wine, and warm eggnog are all traditional drink options that will spice up a party at this time of year. Impress your guests with a well-stocked bar for the occasion (see page 38 for information on stocking a bar).

HORS D'OEUVRES

Cheese Plate
Fruit Plate
Bread Plate
Shrimp Skewers
(page 171)
Nuts
Mini Pastries
Mini Quiches
Miniature Sandwiches

Shrimp and Edamame
Lettuce Cups
(page 160)
Asian-Inspired Meatballs
(page 176)
Grilled Asparagus Tips
Bruschetta
(page 165)
Fried Cheese with Honey

Pick the Music

Four Weeks Before the Party

Spend some time choosing the right music for your party. Make sure you have a lengthy holiday music playlist on your iPod, or burn a few discs for the evening. It is always good to mix in a few traditional holiday tunes for the sake of nostalgia. You can lure your guests into the holiday spirit with songs they are familiar with. You can't go wrong with classic holiday tunes from Tony Bennett, Frank Sinatra, Bing Crosby, or Andy Williams.

HOLIDAY BAR TIPS

- Make sure to have plenty of mixers on hand, including cranberry juice, club soda, Coke, and tonic water.
- Premade concoctions like eggnog or spiked hot cider are great to have on hand. Fill a couple of pitchers with these drinks before your guests arrive.
- Since traditional stemware has gone the way of shoulder pads, consider serving your drinks in Italian-style tumblers. Inexpensive sets of these are available at places like Crate & Barrel or Ikea.
- Be sure you have all the tools you will need to create and serve your specialty drinks, including a corkscrew, muddler, shaker, strainer, and shot glass.
- Provide some nonalcoholic drink options. Have enough mixers on hand so that your guests who don't drink can enjoy "mocktails." Consider having a few nonalcoholic beers on hand as well.
- Variety is key, especially if you are expecting plenty of couples. Women tend to enjoy wine, champagne, and mixed cocktails, while guys tend to prefer beer and single liquor drinks.

Collect the Supplies

Three Weeks Before the Party

As with any party, you should begin collecting the supplies early for your holiday party. You will probably already have many Christmas decorations stored away. If you plan to add a new centerpiece to your collection or hang some garlands, start looking right after Thanksgiving to ensure you have the best selection. Consider buying nonperishable food items early, too. During a regular shopping trip, you can restock spices and other baking items that you may have used up during your Thanksgiving celebration. While out and about, always be on the lookout for different items that might enhance the party's ambience. Look for a new Christmas CD, or check out the special party favors that might be on display. Many stores will have items on sale. If you have access to a specialty store where you can find some unique treasures, remember that this is the season for special treats.

Make the Food

One Week Before the Party

If you are having a casual get-together, you won't need much time to prepare. However, if you are going all out with a sit-down affair, then you should make as much food as you can ahead of time. You can make cookies and pies several weeks in advance and freeze them until the day before the party. To save time when preparing for a full, sit-down dinner, consider buying a prepared ham or turkey. This will allow you to focus on the side dishes and desserts, and leave you plenty of time for the final preparations.

BE A GOOD HOST

Plan ahead. If you're expecting a large gathering, take precautions in the days leading up to your party. Inform your neighbors about the upcoming party, and tour your home to see what rooms might need to be locked during the party hours. Your main job is to encourage the mingling of your guests. If you see them splintering off into high school–type cliques, then it's up to you to loosen up the crowd with some much needed entertainment. You can drink at your own party, but remember to pace yourself. There's no bigger buzzkill then witnessing the hostess slip into an unconscious state at her own party.

GIFT EXCHANGE

There is no need for favors at a holiday party: just ask each guest bring a wrapped present. Set a price limit on the presents and remind your guests to bring generic gifts that can be enjoyed by anyone. Depending on your crowd and the mood of your party, gifts can be either goofy or thoughtful. Place the presents in a pile as the guests arrive. Later in the evening, have each person select a gift. Another option is to coordinate a gift exchange. You can e-mail each guest the name of someone to purchase a gift for. Keep in mind that this only works if all the guests know each other.

Final Preparations

The Day of the Party

You want your guests to mingle at the party. To encourage mingling, set up the bar so that people can make their own drinks. To make things easier, you should still be responsible for preparing any blended drinks. Set up the food and desserts on one side of the room and the drinks on the other to encourage your guests to walk around. You also want your home to smell like the holidays, so fill a baking pan halfway with water and cinnamon and put it in the oven on low heat. This will cause the aromatic smell of cinnamon to fill the house. Also, plug in holiday lights to cheer guests as they arrive at your home, and keep the fire burning in the fireplace to add to the cozy holiday mood.

Remember: this is the season for peace on earth and goodwill toward men. No matter how stressful things get, always take time to enjoy the company of your guests. Work to make things perfect up until your guests arrive, and then let go and enjoy the party.

Part 3

The Recipes

- fourteen -

Appetizers

Bacon-Wrapped Dates
Serves 15 (3 per person)

23 slices center-cut bacon

45 whole pitted dates

Toothpicks

Freshly cracked black pepper

Cut the bacon slices in half using kitchen scissors. Wrap one slice of bacon around each date and secure it with a toothpick. Repeat with the remaining slices of bacon and dates. (You will have one slice of bacon leftover.)

Arrange the bacon-wrapped dates in a single layer in a large skillet or griddle pan and place on the stovetop over medium heat. Cook until the bacon is caramelized on all sides, using the toothpicks to turn the dates. This will take about 10 minutes. Remove from the heat and sprinkle with freshly cracked black pepper.

Gouda and Cantaloupe
Serves 15 (3 per person)

1 cup balsamic vinegar

5 tablespoons granulated sugar

¼ cup water

24 ounces Gouda cheese, cut into 1-inch cubes
   (you will need about 45 cubes total)

½ cantaloupe, cubed or balled (you will need about 45)

45 basil leaves (approximately 2 large bunches)

Toothpicks

Combine the balsamic vinegar, sugar, and water in a small saucepan and cook over medium heat until thickened and reduced to ½ cup, about 30 minutes. While this cooks, spear a piece of cheese, cantaloupe, and basil leaf with a toothpick. Repeat with the remaining ingredients. Drizzle the Gouda and cantaloupe with the cooled balsamic vinegar reduction.

Guacamole
Serves 15

4 avocados, cut into small chunks

4 Roma tomatoes, diced

1 cup onion, chopped

Juice of 2 limes

1 teaspoon salt

¼ cup light sour cream (optional)

½ cup cilantro leaves

Combine the avocados, tomatoes, onion, lime juice, and salt in a large bowl. Gently smash the avocados, leaving some larger chunks. Mix in the sour cream if desired. Sprinkle cilantro on top.

Pita Chips and White Bean Dip
Serves 15

4 14-ounce cans cannellini or Great Northern beans,
   drained and rinsed

1 teaspoon minced garlic

1 tablespoon plus 1 teaspoon lemon zest

1 tablespoon plus 1 teaspoon lemon juice

1 tablespoon plus 1 teaspoon fresh rosemary, chopped

2 teaspoons salt

Freshly cracked black pepper

Tabasco sauce to taste

6 tablespoons extra-virgin olive oil

½ cup sun-dried tomatoes, chopped

2 18-ounce bags of pita chips

Combine the beans, garlic, lemon zest, lemon juice, rosemary, salt, pepper, and Tabasco sauce in a food processor and process until smooth and creamy. Drizzle the olive oil over the mixture while the food processor is running. Fold in the sun-dried tomatoes just before serving. Serve with pita chips.

Shrimp and Edamame Lettuce Cups

Serves 15 (1 per person)

30 medium shrimp, peeled and deveined

15 whole butter lettuce leaves, rinsed and dried

4 cups Napa cabbage, shredded

2 cups edamame (soybeans), shelled

1 red bell pepper, diced

½ cup ground honey-roasted peanuts

Freshly cracked pepper

If the shrimp is not precooked, prep your shrimp the day before the party. Fill a medium saucepan with water and place over medium-high heat. When the water has reached a gentle boil, turn the heat down to medium and place the shrimp in the water for about 3 minutes until cooked. Immediately remove the shrimp to an ice water bath to halt the cooking process. Drain and store in a covered container in the refrigerator.

To assemble the salad cups, arrange the butter lettuce leaves in a single layer on a large platter. Combine the cabbage and edamame in a large bowl, and scoop equal amounts of the mixture into each lettuce leaf. Place two shrimp on top of each salad, then sprinkle red bell pepper, peanuts, and freshly cracked pepper on top. Serve with a choice of salad dressings.

Miso Honey Dressing

Makes about ⅔ cup

½ cup white low-sodium miso paste

¼ cup honey

Juice of 2 limes

2 tablespoons rice vinegar

2 garlic cloves, smashed

¼ cup cilantro leaves

Freshly cracked black pepper

Salt, optional

Combine the miso paste, honey, lime juice, rice vinegar, and garlic in a food processor. Pulse until smooth and combined, about 1 minute. Add the cilantro and pulse a few more times. Season to taste with freshly cracked pepper, adding additional lime juice, honey, or salt if needed.

Pomelo Cilantro Lime Vinaigrette

Makes about 1 cup

1 cup freshly squeezed pomelo juice

   (you can also use oroblanco or grapefruit juice)

Juice of 2 limes

½ cup cilantro, finely chopped

½ to 1 teaspoon granulated sugar

3 tablespoons extra-virgin olive oil

Salt and pepper

In a medium bowl, whisk together the pomelo and lime juices. Add the cilantro and ½ teaspoon sugar and whisk well. Drizzle in the olive oil one tablespoon at a time, whisking thoroughly after each addition. Season with salt and pepper to taste, adding additional sugar if desired.

Sour Cream Dip
Serves 12

⅔ cup dill, loosely packed

16 ounces light sour cream

2 tablespoons honey mustard

2 teaspoons red pepper flakes

½ teaspoon sea salt

Finely chop the dill. Mix with sour cream, honey mustard, red pepper flakes, and sea salt. Serve with vegetables or whole-grain crackers.

Pizza Pinwheels
Makes 14

Nonstick cooking spray

1 sheet frozen puff pastry, thawed

3 tomatoes, seeded and thinly sliced

30 slices pepperoni (about half of a 6-ounce package)

1 cup mozzarella cheese, grated

⅓ cup basil chiffonade

Preheat the oven to 350°F. Lightly coat a cookie sheet with nonstick cooking spray. Roll out the puff pastry and cover with an even layer of a tomato slices followed by a layer of pepperoni. Add a layer of grated cheese over the pepperoni and sprinkle with the basil. Gently lift up the bottom of pastry and roll tightly. Using a serrated knife, cut into ½-inch slices. Arrange the pizza pinwheels on the prepared cookie sheet. Bake for 15 minutes at 350°F, then turn the heat up to 400°F and bake for an additional 5 minutes, until lightly browned.

Bruschetta

Serves 8 (2 per person)

6 tablespoons extra-virgin olive oil

3 garlic cloves, minced

1 baguette, sliced diagonally into 16 1-inch-thick slices

12 ounces mozzarella cheese, sliced thinly into 16 slices

2 pounds Roma tomatoes (about 8 tomatoes), seeded and diced

½ cup fresh basil chiffonade

Sea salt

Preheat the oven to 200°F. In a small bowl, combine the olive oil and garlic and let it sit for 30 minutes to allow the garlic to fully infuse the oil. Lightly brush the garlic oil on both sides of the bread slices and arrange on a cookie sheet. Place a slice of mozzarella on top of each piece of bread and bake for about 10 minutes, until the cheese begins to soften. Mix 1 tablespoon of the remaining garlic oil with the tomatoes, fresh basil, and sea salt. Spoon about 2 tablespoons of the tomato mixture on top of the cheese.

Pinwheels

Makes 18

6 large (10- to 12-inch) tortilla wraps

¾ cup hummus

3 cups spinach

18 slices center-cut bacon, cooked

24 slices turkey

3 tomatoes, seeded and thinly sliced

1½ avocado, sliced

Spread 2 tablespoons hummus on each tortilla. Place a layer of spinach on the hummus, followed by 3 slices of bacon and 4 slices of turkey. Divide the tomato and avocado slices evenly among the tortillas. Fold in the sides about ½-inch and roll tightly into wraps. Secure the wraps with 3 toothpicks, placing one in the middle and one on each side. Cut into thirds with a serrated knife.

Black Bean and Corn Nachos
Serves 10

1 9-ounce package multigrain tortilla chips

1½ 8-ounce packages reduced fat cheddar jack cheese, shredded

1 15.5-ounce can black beans, drained

2 cups fresh corn

2 tomatoes, diced

2 avocados, cut into small chunks

1 cup sour cream

5 jalapeños, sliced

Lime wedges

Preheat the oven to 350°F. Line two baking sheets with tortilla chips. Sprinkle the cheese on top of the chips. Sprinkle the black beans and corn on top of the cheese. Place in the oven and bake until the cheese melts, 5 to 10 minutes. Remove from oven and top with tomatoes and avocados. Serve with sour cream, jalapeños, and lime wedges.

Hot Crab Dip
Serves 10 to 12

1 8-ounce package reduced fat cream cheese at room temperature

½ cup canola oil mayonnaise

1 teaspoon crawfish boil seasoning

¼ teaspoon paprika

¼ teaspoon garlic powder

¼ teaspoon red pepper flakes

5 ounces fresh lump crabmeat

2 stalks green onion, thinly sliced

French bread cut into 1-inch slices or crackers for serving

Preheat the oven to 350°F. Place the cream cheese and mayonnaise in a mixing bowl and beat on low speed until combined. Add the crawfish boil seasoning, paprika, garlic powder, and red pepper flakes to the mixture and beat until blended. Using a spatula, fold in the crabmeat and green onions until evenly distributed. Spread the mixture in an 8-inch square baking dish. Bake for 15 minutes. Serve with French bread or crackers.

Chicken Nuggets
Serves 15 (about 3 per person)

Canola oil

2 cups flour

2 teaspoons salt

2 teaspoons seasoned salt

4 eggs, beaten

8 ounces panko bread crumbs

2¼ pounds chicken tenders, cut into thirds

Pour canola oil into a large skillet until oil is ½-inch deep and place the skillet over medium-high heat. While the oil is heating, combine the flour, salt, and seasoned salt in a bowl. Pour the eggs into a second bowl. Place the panko bread crumbs in a third bowl. The oil is ready when a pinch of flour sputters in the skillet. Dip the chicken nuggets, one at a time, first into the flour mixture, then into the egg, then into the panko bread crumbs. Cook in the hot oil for about 3 minutes on each side, until done. You may have to cook the nuggets in batches, depending on the size of your skillet.

Pigs in a Blanket
Serves 6 (4 per person)

1 teaspoon canola oil

1 cup sliced onions

14 ounces turkey sausage (2 large links)

3 8-ounce packages reduced fat crescent rolls

Preheat the oven to 350°F. Heat the canola oil in a sauté pan over medium heat. When the oil is hot, add the onions and cook until caramelized, about 5 minutes. Remove from the heat and set aside.

Cut each turkey sausage link into thirds widthwise. Then cut each third into quarters lengthwise. You should have 24 sausage pieces total. Roll each piece of sausage with a small amount of onions into a piece of crescent dough. Bake on an ungreased cookie sheet for about 10 minutes, then turn them over and bake for another 3 minutes.

Shrimp Wontons
Serves 15 (about 3 per person)

45 jumbo shrimp (about 2 pounds), shelled and cooked

2 bunches green onion, each cut about 2 inches long

2 8.8-ounce boxes of egg roll wrappers

Canola oil

Wrap each shrimp along with a piece of green onion in an egg roll wrapper. Pour canola oil into a large skillet until oil is ½-inch deep and heat over medium-high heat. The oil is hot enough when a pinch of flour sizzles in the skillet. Fry the wontons until golden brown, about 2 minutes per side.

Shrimp Skewers

Serves 15 (3 per person)

½ cup low-sodium soy sauce

1½ tablespoons granulated sugar

2 teaspoons sesame oil

3 teaspoons ginger, grated

¼ cup (about 1 bunch) green onion, minced

45 large shrimp (about 1½ pounds), peeled and deveined

Wood skewers

Combine the soy sauce, sugar, oil, ginger, and green onion in a large bowl. Add the shrimp and marinate for at least 30 minutes and up to 2 hours. Thread the shrimp on wood skewers, taking care not to crowd the shrimp. Heat a grill to medium-hot and cook the shrimp for about 2 minutes per side, until done.

Trail Mix

Serves 15

5 cups Wheat Chex cereal

2 cups honey-roasted peanuts

2 cups dried apple rings

1 cup dark chocolate candies

Combine all ingredients and serve in decorative bowls.

Vegetarian Egg Rolls
Makes 70

3 tablespoons canola oil, divided, plus more for frying

½ block firm tofu, sliced into ½-inch cubes

1 cup straw mushrooms (drained if canned)

2 cups cabbage, thinly sliced

1 yellow onion, roughly chopped

1 large carrot, roughly chopped

1 leek, roughly chopped

1 tablespoon sugar

1 teaspoon pepper

1½ tablespoons soy sauce

3 eggs, divided

¼ teaspoon salt

2 50-count packages of 4x5-inch spring roll pastry wrappers

Heat 2 tablespoons canola oil in a sauté pan over medium-high heat. When the oil is hot, fry the tofu until golden, about 3 minutes per side. Place in a food processor. Add the straw mushrooms, cabbage, yellow onion, carrots, and leeks. Process until the vegetables are well chopped and the tofu looks like cottage cheese curds. Transfer the tofu mixture to a mixing bowl and add the sugar, pepper, salt, soy sauce, 1 tablespoon canola oil, and two of the eggs. Beat the other egg in a small dish and set aside.

Spoon a tablespoon of tofu mixture in the middle of each spring roll wrapper. Put a dab of beaten egg on the top point of the spring roll wrapper. Fold up the opposite point and roll toward the top. Carefully fold in the sides of the wrapper as you roll, and seal the edge with another dab of egg. You will have about 30 spring roll wrappers leftover.

Fill a frying pan with ¼-inch of canola oil or enough to cover ¾ of an egg roll, and place over high heat. When the oil is shimmering hot, reduce the heat to medium and fry the spring rolls in batches until golden brown, about 5 minutes per side.

How-to photos on the next page

Asian-Inspired Meatballs
Makes 30 meatballs

1 pound ground pork

1¼ pounds lean ground turkey

5 garlic cloves, minced and divided

1 tablespoon plus 1 teaspoon ginger, grated

1 large onion, finely diced and divided

¾ cup cilantro, finely chopped and divided

¼ cup green onion, thinly sliced

2 tablespoons light soy sauce

1 tablespoon plus 1 teaspoon sugar

1 teaspoon freshly grated black pepper

About 6 tablespoons extra-virgin olive oil, divided

1 15-ounce can tomato sauce

1 28-ounce can peeled whole tomatoes

1 teaspoon crushed red pepper

1 tablespoon sesame oil

½ cup water

In a large bowl, mix together the ground pork, ground turkey, 4 of the garlic cloves, 1 tablespoon ginger, half of the onion, ¼ cup of the cilantro, green onion, soy sauce, sugar, pepper, and 1 tablespoon extra-virgin olive oil. Form into 30 meatball patties, about 2 tablespoons each or the size of golf balls. Pour 2 tablespoons of olive oil into a large frying pan. In two batches, cook the meatballs over medium heat until golden brown, about 5 minutes per side. Add more olive oil to the pan for the second batch if needed. Transfer to a plate when done.

Heat 1 tablespoon of olive oil in a 5½-quart Dutch oven over medium heat. Sauté the remaining garlic clove and teaspoon of ginger along with the rest of the onion. Pour in the tomato sauce and peeled whole tomatoes, breaking up the whole tomatoes with a spatula. Mix in the crushed red pepper and sesame oil. Add the water, and gently stir in the meatballs. Cook over medium-low heat for 30 minutes. Stir in the remaining ½ cup cilantro before serving.

Soft Pretzels
Serves 8

2¼-ounce packages active dry yeast

2 cups warm water (between 110°F and 115°F)

½ cup light brown sugar, divided

3 teaspoons salt

6½ cups all-purpose flour

¼ cup butter, softened

Nonstick cooking spray

2 teaspoons baking soda

2 teaspoons hot water

1 egg, beaten

Coarse salt

Dissolve the yeast in the warm water. Add 1 tablespoon of the sugar. Allow the yeast mixture to sit for 5 minutes to activate. The liquid should be foamy. Next, add the remaining sugar, salt, flour, and butter. Mix with a wooden spoon until a smooth dough forms. If the dough seems too dry, add a tablespoon of water. Knead the dough for about 5 minutes. Transfer to a bowl coated with cooking spray and cover with plastic wrap coated with cooking spray. Let the dough rest in the refrigerator for 2 to 24 hours.

Grease a large baking sheet. Transfer the dough to a lightly floured surface. Punch down the dough and divide in half. Cut each half into 12 pieces and roll each piece into a long rope. Form the rope into a pretzel shape. Place the pretzels on the baking sheet, cover, and let rise in a warm place for 30 minutes or until doubled in size. While the pretzels are rising, preheat the oven to 400°F.

Combine the baking soda and hot water. Dip the pretzels in the baking soda mixture and then brush them with the remaining egg. Sprinkle each pretzel with coarse salt and bake for 15 minutes or until golden brown.

Note: Instead of salt, experiment with different toppings for the pretzels, such as sesame seeds, poppy seeds, caraway seeds, or a mixture of ground peppers for spicy pretzels.

- fifteen -

Soups and Sandwiches

Leek and Potato Soup

Makes 10 cups

2 tablespoons canola oil

2 potatoes (about 2¼ pounds),
    peeled and sliced into 8 rounds each

1 leek (about 2½ cups), thinly sliced

1 quart (32 ounces) low-sodium chicken broth

1 cup water

2 cups reduced fat milk

2 teaspoons salt

½ teaspoon pepper

Heat the canola oil in a 5-quart soup pot over medium-high heat. Add the potatoes and leeks and sauté for 5 minutes, until the leeks are slightly softened. Add the chicken broth and water, reduce heat to medium, and simmer for about 25 minutes, until the potatoes are fork-tender. Remove from the heat and add the milk, stirring to combine.

Carefully pour the soup into a large bowl or pot. Working in small batches, purée the soup in a blender. Do not fill the blender more than two-thirds full or the steam will blow the lid off. Pour the puréed soup back into the original soup pot. Continue until all the soup is puréed. Add salt and pepper to taste. Reheat the soup over medium heat until simmering and serve hot.

Chicken Burgers
Serves 15 (1 per person)

1 stalk lemongrass

3 tablespoons fish sauce

1½ teaspoons low-sodium soy sauce

9 garlic cloves, minced

3 teaspoons granulated sugar

¾ teaspoons turmeric powder

1½ teaspoons red pepper flakes

4½ pounds boneless chicken thighs (about 15 thighs), fat trimmed*

¼ cup canola oil, divided

15 mini baguettes, halved

Canola oil mayonnaise

Arugula or spinach

Cut off the bottom of the lemongrass stalk, peel off the tough outer layers, and mince the tender leaves inside. You should have about 9 tablespoons of minced lemongrass. Combine the lemongrass, fish sauce, soy sauce, garlic, sugar, turmeric, and red pepper flakes in a large bowl. Add the chicken thighs, cover, and let marinate in the refrigerator for 1 to 2 hours.

Heat 2 tablespoon of canola oil in a large skillet over medium-high heat. Fry the chicken thighs in two batches, about 6 minutes per side, until done.

To assemble the burgers, spread canola oil mayonnaise on the bottom halves of the baguette slices. Add some arugula or spinach, place a chicken thigh on top, and cover with the top halves of the baguettes.

*If you can't find boneless chicken thighs at your grocery store, ask the butcher to bone the thighs for you.

Mini Barbeque Turkey Sliders on Brioche Buns

Serves 15 (2 per serving)

2½ pounds ground turkey

½ cup barbeque sauce

1 teaspoon kosher salt

1 teaspoon black pepper

2 teaspoons red pepper flakes

½ teaspoon horseradish

30 mini brioche buns

5 to 6 plum tomatoes, sliced

Arugula

Gourmet mustard

Mayonnaise (combined with a pinch of saffron, optional)

Optional condiments: avocado, sun-dried tomatoes, roasted bell
    pepper strips

Preheat a gas grill or prepare a charcoal grill and brush the grate lightly with oil. In a large bowl, combine the ground turkey, barbeque sauce, salt, black pepper, red pepper flakes, and horseradish. Form 30 burger patties (about ¼ cup each), and grill each side for a few minutes until done. Place the burgers on the buns.

To serve, arrange the burgers on a plate and cover them with a cotton kitchen towel to keep them warm. Place the arugula leaves and other condiments on a plate, or in small bowls to the side. Let your guests assemble their brioche burgers to their liking.

Ultimate Hamburgers
Serves 6

1 pound lean ground beef

1 egg, beaten

¼ cup whole grain bread crumbs

1 cup yellow onion, diced

¼ teaspoon sea salt

½ teaspoon black pepper

Whole grain or white hamburger buns

Cheese

Spinach or lettuce

Tomato

Heat a clean grill to medium hot, so that you are able to hold your hand six inches from the grate for only a second or two. Combine the ground beef, egg, bread crumbs, onion, salt, and pepper in a mixing bowl and mix until just combined. Measure out ½ cup portions of beef and form into balls, then flatten to your desired thickness. Make an indentation in the center of each patty to keep the burger from shrinking during cooking.

When the grill is hot, add the beef patties and shut the grill, making sure the vents are open. Cook the patties on one side for 6 to 10 minutes. The degree to which the burgers are cooked—rare, medium, or well done—will vary with the cooking time. Open the grill, flip the patties, and close the lid. Cook for another 6 to 10 minutes.

Place the cooked burgers on buns and dress with cheese, spinach or lettuce, tomato, and various other condiments.

Variations:

Ultimate Bacon Avocado Burger
Slice 1 avocado and cook 8 slices of bacon. Top each burger with 2 avocado slices and 2 strips of bacon.

Ultimate Bleu Cheese Burger

Add a teaspoon of Worcestershire sauce and a teaspoon of dry mustard to the ground beef mixture before cooking. Top each burger with 1 ounce of crumbled bleu cheese.

Ultimate Mushroom Swiss Burger

Slice 12 ounces of shiitake or button mushrooms. Heat 3 tablespoons butter in pan over medium-high heat and cook the mushrooms for 8 minutes or until very soft. Sprinkle with a teaspoon of coarse salt. Divide among the burgers and top with a slice of Swiss cheese.

Veggie Burgers
Serves 4

1 15-ounce can garbanzo beans

¼ cup whole grain bread crumbs

1 egg

¼ cup cilantro

¼ teaspoon cumin

¼ teaspoon sea salt

2 tablespoons canola oil

Whole grain or white hamburger buns

Spinach or lettuce

Sliced onions

Tomato

In the bowl of a food processor, combine the garbanzo beans, bread crumbs, egg, cilantro, cumin, and sea salt. Process until the mixture is puréed and resembles hummus. Roll ¼-cup portions into balls and flatten to your desired thickness. Heat the oil in a large frying pan over medium heat and cook the patties for about 5 minutes per side. Place the cooked veggie burgers on buns and dress with spinach or lettuce, onions, tomato, and various other condiments.

sixteen

Entrées

Turkey and Veggie Lasagna
Serves 10 to 12

1 16-ounce package of lasagna

8 ounces mushrooms, sliced

1 cup carrots, peeled and sliced

1 cup celery, sliced

1 small green zucchini, cut in half lengthwise and sliced into ¼-inch-thick pieces

1 small yellow squash, cut in half lengthwise and sliced into ¼-inch-thick pieces

½ red bell pepper, sliced

½ green bell pepper, sliced

½ small onion, chopped

3 tablespoons extra-virgin olive oil, divided

¾ teaspoon black pepper, divided

¾ teaspoon sugar, divided

1 tablespoon plus 1½ teaspoons soy sauce

64 ounces pasta sauce

4 garlic cloves, minced

1¼ pounds extra lean ground turkey

½ teaspoon salt

Continued on the next page

1 tablespoon fennel seeds

1 tablespoon fresh thyme

1 tablespoon crushed red pepper

3 cups mozzarella or cheddar cheese, shredded

Bring a large 4-quart pot of water to a boil. Add the lasagna and cook for 5 to 7 minutes until the noodles are al dente. Drain the noodles and set aside.

Pour 1 tablespoon of olive oil in a sauté pan and place over high heat. In the pan, combine the mushrooms, carrots, celery, zucchini, squash, red bell pepper, green bell pepper, onion, ¼ teaspoon black pepper, ¼ teaspoon sugar, and ½ teaspoon soy sauce. Cook for 10 minutes, stirring frequently. When the carrots are tender, drain the vegetables, keeping them in the pan. Add the pasta sauce to the vegetables and set aside.

Heat the remaining 2 tablespoons of olive oil in a large pan over medium-high heat. Add the garlic and ground turkey and stir to break the turkey into crumbles. Sprinkle with the remaining ½ teaspoon sugar and ½ teaspoon black pepper. Add 1 teaspoon of soy sauce, salt, fennel, thyme, and crushed red pepper. Cook for about 8 minutes, until the turkey is completely cooked.

Add the cooked turkey to the vegetables in the pan. Add the remaining 1 tablespoon soy sauce and cook over medium heat for another 20 minutes.

Preheat the oven to 350°F. Arrange the lasagna noodles in a single layer in a 13x9-inch baking dish. Add a layer of the vegetable-meat mixture and top with ¾ cup cheese. Repeat for two more layers, finishing with the cheese. Bake for 30 minutes at 350°F, then set the oven to broil and bake for about 8 minutes, until the cheese turns golden brown.

Pork Tenderloin with Mango Chutney

Serves 12 to 16

4 tablespoons olive oil

1 cup store-bought mango ginger chutney

6 tablespoons brown sugar

Juice of 1 lime

6 garlic cloves, chopped

1 tablespoon cumin

1 teaspoon black pepper

1 teaspoon chili powder

1 tablespoon sea salt

4 pork tenderloins (about 5 pounds total)

1 cup water

Preheat the oven to 350°F. Combine the oil, chutney, brown sugar, lime juice, garlic, cumin, pepper, chili powder, and sea salt in a large baking dish. Add the pork tenderloins and turn to coat all sides with the mixture. Allow to marinade for about 15 minutes.

Heat a large, ovenproof sauté pan over high heat until very hot. Reserving the marinade in a separate container, sear the tenderloins in the pan until browned on all sides, 2 to 3 minutes per side. Place the pan into the oven and roast for 22 to 25 minutes, until the meat is slightly pink and a meat thermometer inserted into the center of the tenderloins registers 155° F to 160°F. Take the pork out of the oven and allow it to rest a few minutes before cutting.

While the pork is roasting, combine the reserved marinade with the water in a small saucepan. Bring to a boil while stirring, then lower the heat to medium-low and simmer for 6 to 7 minutes, until the sauce is slightly reduced. Ladle over the pork tenderloins to serve.

Vegetarian Curry

Serves 12 to 15

3 tablespoons vegetable oil

2 teaspoons chili oil

4 garlic cloves, crushed

2 stalks lemongrass, each cut into 3 pieces and bruised

2 12-ounce block of extra firm tofu, cubed

16 ounces whole button mushrooms

2 sweet potatoes (about 2 pounds), peeled and cubed

4 small purple Okinawan sweet potatoes (about 1½ pounds), peeled and cubed (or use an additional 2 regular sweet potatoes)

2 cups baby carrots

5 tablespoons Madras curry powder

2 to 4 dried red chilies, soaked in water and sliced

4 kaffir lime leaves

2 cups coconut milk

4 cups water

4 cups vegetable broth

2 tablespoons soy sauce

Sea salt

2 cups Thai basil leaves, torn (or use cilantro if preferred)

In a large soup pot over medium-high heat, combine the vegetable oil and chili oil. When the oil is hot, add the garlic and lemongrass and sauté for 2 to 3 minutes. Add the tofu and mushrooms and fry for 2 to 3 minutes on each side, until lightly browned. Transfer the tofu mixture to a separate bowl and set aside.

Add a little more oil to the pot, if needed. Fry the sweet potatoes, purple potatoes, and carrots for 6 to 7 minutes, until potatoes are lightly browned. Return the tofu mixture to the pot and sprinkle with the curry powder. Stir until the curry powder is well incorporated, then add the red chilies and lime leaves.

Continued on the next page

Reduce the heat to medium. Add the coconut milk, water, broth, and soy sauce to the pot and bring to a light boil. Adjust the taste by adding extra sea salt or soy sauce. Reduce the heat to medium low and simmer for 25 to 30 minutes, uncovered.

To serve, ladle the curry into shallow bowls and top with basil leaves.

Old-Fashioned Stuffing
Serves 8

1 large loaf of stale, crusty bread

4 tablespoons butter

1 large onion, chopped

3 celery stalks, chopped

1 teaspoon dried sage

1 teaspoon dried rosemary

½ teaspoon coarse salt

Freshly ground black pepper

16 ounces chicken stock

Preheat the oven to 350°F and grease a 13x9-inch baking dish. Gently crush the bread with a meat tenderizer or rolling pin and collect the crumbs in a large bowl. Melt the butter in a heavy skillet over medium heat. Add the onion and celery and cook, stirring frequently, until soft, about 15 minutes. Add the vegetables to the large bowl of bread crumbs and set aside.

Pour the chicken stock into the skillet and turn the heat to medium-low. Add the sage, rosemary, salt, and black pepper and stir to mix. Add the hot chicken stock to the bread crumb mixture in the bowl in ½ cup increments, stirring after each addition until well mixed. Transfer to the prepared baking dish, cover with foil, and bake for 30 minutes. Uncover and bake for an additional 12 minutes or until the top is golden brown.

Vegetarian Chili

Serves 8 to 10

2 tablespoons extra-virgin olive oil

½ large onion, diced

4 garlic cloves, minced

1 red bell pepper, diced

1 15.5-ounce can Great Northern beans, drained

1 15.5-ounce can kidney beans, drained

1 28-ounce can crushed tomatoes

1 tablespoon plus 1 teaspoon chili powder

1 tablespoon cumin

1 teaspoon red pepper flakes

2 cups low-sodium vegetable broth

Salt

In a stockpot, heat the oil over medium-high heat and sauté the onions and garlic for about 5 minutes. Add the red bell pepper and sauté for another 2 minutes. Add the Great Northern beans, kidney beans, tomatoes, chili powder, cumin, red pepper flakes, and vegetable broth. Bring to a boil, then reduce the heat to low. Cook for 1 hour. Add salt to taste.

Dry Rub Salmon
Serves 4

2 tablespoons brown sugar

2 teaspoons salt-free grilling spice blend

¼ teaspoon cayenne pepper

¼ teaspoon freshly ground black pepper

½ teaspoon sea salt

Cooking spray

1¼ pounds fresh salmon

Preheat the oven to 325°F. In a small bowl, combine the brown sugar, grilling spices, cayenne pepper, black pepper, and sea salt. Spray the inside of a jelly roll pan with cooking spray and place the salmon in the pan. Spread half of the spice mixture on the skin side of the salmon. Flip the salmon over and repeat on the other side. Bake for 15 to 18 minutes, until the fish flakes easily with a fork.

Shrimp and Cucumber Pasta
Serves 8

1 pound large shrimp, shelled and deveined

1 12-ounce box whole wheat penne pasta

1½ cups frozen soybeans or green peas

1 English cucumber

½ cup extra-virgin olive oil

Juice of 1½ lemons

½ teaspoon sea salt

⅓ cup capers, drained

½ cup dill leaves, finely chopped

½ teaspoon freshly ground black pepper

Fill two large pots halfway with water and place over high heat. When water boils, add the shrimp to one pot and the pasta to the other. Cook the shrimp for about 4 minutes, or until opaque. Drain the shrimp and immediately place in an ice water bath to halt the cooking process. Drain again. Cook the pasta according to box directions. Drain the pasta and set aside.

In a medium saucepan, bring 3 cups of water to a boil over medium-high heat. Add the frozen peas or soybeans and cook for 3 minutes, then drain. Combine the cooled pasta, shrimp, and soybeans in a large bowl.

Slice the English cucumber in ¼-inch thick round pieces, then cut in half to make semicircles. In a small bowl, whisk together the olive oil, lemon juice, and sea salt. Pour this mixture over the pasta and shrimp. Stir in the cucumber, capers, chopped dill leaves, and ground pepper. Cool in the refrigerator before serving.

Herb-Roasted Turkey
Serves 12

1 12-pound turkey

2 tablespoons garlic powder

3 teaspoons dried sage

1 teaspoon dried rosemary

1 teaspoon basil

1 teaspoon oregano

2 teaspoons coarse salt

1 teaspoon black pepper

10 garlic cloves, peeled

1 cup vegetable oil

2 cups water

Preheat the oven to 325°F. Clean the turkey, discarding any giblets. In a small bowl, combine the garlic powder, sage, rosemary, basil, oregano, salt, and pepper. Use a paring knife to make evenly spaced slits in the bird and insert the garlic cloves into the slits. Carefully separate the skin from the bird with a small paring knife. Rub the spice mixture under the skin. Don't worry if the skin separates from the bird or tears. Replace it as well as you can.

Place the turkey breast side up on a roasting rack. Rub the outside of the turkey with vegetable oil. Add the water to the bottom of the pan, cover, and bake for 2½ hours. Uncover and bake for an additional ½ hour, or until the internal temperature at the thigh reaches 180°F.

Sweet Potato Casserole
Serves 6 to 8

2½ pounds sweet potatoes

¼ cup maple syrup

½ cup dark brown sugar

¾ cup unsalted pecans, halved (or ½ cup ground pecans)

½ cup white whole wheat flour

1 teaspoon cinnamon

¼ teaspoon nutmeg

⅓ cup cold unsalted butter, cut into tablespoons

Place the sweet potatoes, whole, in a large pot of boiling water and cook until fork-tender, then drain and allow to cool. Preheat the oven to 350°F.

Peel the cooled potatoes and cut into 1-inch thick round slices. Cut the slices in half and place in a large bowl. Drizzle the potatoes with the maple syrup, toss to coat, and place in an 8-inch square baking dish.

In the work bowl of a food processor or a large bowl, combine the brown sugar, pecans, flour, cinnamon, and nutmeg. Cut in the butter and process (or work together with a pastry cutter or two knives) until the mixture resembles small pebbles. Sprinkle the pecan mixture on top of sweet potatoes and bake for 30 minutes.

Sautéed Green Beans
Serves 4

1 tablespoon extra-virgin olive oil

2 garlic cloves

12 ounces green beans

¼ cup unsalted chicken broth

Salt and pepper

In a large saucepan, heat the oil over medium-high heat and sauté the garlic for 2 to 3 minutes. Add the green beans and sauté for an additional 3 minutes. Add the chicken broth, bring to a simmer, and cook the green beans until tender, about 3 minutes. Season to taste with salt and pepper.

Roasted Root Vegetables
Serves 8

2 large sweet potatoes

5 small carrots

6 red potatoes (about 1½ pounds)

4 small turnips

3 tablespoons extra-virgin olive oil

½ teaspoon sea salt

2 tablespoons fresh rosemary, finely chopped

½ teaspoon freshly ground black pepper

Preheat oven to 425°F. Peel the sweet potatoes and cut them into 1-inch cubes. Peel the carrots and cut them into thirds. Quarter the red potatoes, leaving the skins on. Peel and quarter the turnips. Toss the vegetable with the extra-virgin olive oil, sea salt, rosemary, and black pepper. Transfer to a baking dish and roast for about 50 minutes, until vegetables are fork-tender.

Roasted Brussels Sprouts
Serves 6

1 pound Brussels sprouts

2 tablespoons olive oil

½ teaspoon sea salt

Freshly ground black pepper

4 slices center-cut bacon, cooked and crumbled

Preheat the oven to 400°F. Cut each Brussels sprout into thirds. Place them in a large bowl and drizzle with the olive oil. Sprinkle with the sea salt, add pepper to taste, and toss to coat thoroughly. Arrange the Brussels sprouts on a cookie sheet and roast for 5 minutes, then flip them over and roast for an additional 5 minutes, until they begin to brown. Sprinkle with crumbled bacon before serving.

Potato Pancakes
Serves 8

2 pounds Yukon Gold potatoes

1 large onion, grated

¼ cup parsley, finely chopped

1 teaspoon salt

1 teaspoon baking powder

1 large egg, beaten

3 tablespoons all-purpose flour

Vegetable oil

Peel and grate the potatoes. Combine the grated potatoes, onion, and parsley in a dish towel and wring out the water. In a large bowl, combine the potato mixture with the salt, baking powder, egg, and flour. Stir with a wooden spoon until well mixed. Fill a large cast iron skillet with 2 inches of oil and place over medium heat. When hot, add ¼ cup scoops of the potato mixture to the pan, taking care not to crowd them. Flatten the pancakes with a spatula and cook for about 5 minutes per side, or until golden brown.

Herb-Roasted New Potatoes
Serves 12 to 14

5 pounds new potatoes

1¼ teaspoons sea salt

1¼ teaspoons freshly ground black pepper

2 ½ teaspoon fresh thyme, chopped

¼ cup extra-virgin olive oil

Preheat the oven to 375°F. Thoroughly wash the potatoes, keeping the skins on, quarter them, and transfer to a large bowl. Sprinkle the salt, pepper, and thyme on the potatoes. Add the olive oil and toss to coat. Arrange the potatoes on a large cookie sheet (or two, if necessary to avoid crowding them). Bake for 45 minutes, stirring the potatoes after about 20 minutes, until fork-tender.

Home-Style Mashed Potatoes
Serves 8

6 large russet potatoes, peeled and cubed

6 tablespoons butter

½ cup half-and-half, divided

1 teaspoon coarse salt

Black pepper

Boil the potatoes in a large pot with enough water to cover them. Cook for 25 minutes, or until fork-tender. Drain well and return to the pot. Add the butter and ¼ cup half-and-half and mash with a potato masher until the potatoes are broken up. Add the remaining half-and-half, salt, and pepper to taste. Continue mashing until fluffy.

seventeen

Desserts

Apple Galette
Serves 6 to 8

3 apples, peeled, cored, and sliced into ¼-inch thick slices

Juice of ½ lemon

¼ cup brown sugar

¼ cup granulated sugar

¼ teaspoon cinnamon (Roasted Saigon Cinnamon is best)

1 tablespoon all-purpose flour

1 sheet frozen puff pastry, thawed

1 egg, beaten

Preheat the oven to 350°F. In a medium bowl, mix together the apples, lemon juice, brown sugar, granulated sugar, cinnamon, and flour. Roll out the puff pastry, using flour as necessary to keep it from sticking to surfaces, and place the apple mixture in the center. Fold the sides of the puff pastry up, covering some of the apples, and place on a cookie sheet. Brush the egg over exposed pastry.

Bake in the oven for 10 minutes at 350°F, then increase the temperature to 375°F and bake for an additional 10 to 15 minutes, until a fork inserted into the apples pierces them easily and the crust is golden brown.

Yogurt Petits Fours with Coconut Icing

Serves 20 (3 1-inch petits fours per person)

Petits Fours

7 tablespoons unsalted butter, at room temperature

¾ cup granulated sugar

2 eggs, at room temperature

1¼ cups all-purpose flour (stir the flour before scooping into
    measuring cup)

¼ cup cornstarch

1 teaspoon baking soda

¼ teaspoon salt

½ cup skim milk

½ cup fat-free plain yogurt

1 teaspoon vanilla extract

Edible gold dragées

Mini gold foil cupcake liners

Coconut Icing

8 cups powdered sugar

1 cup coconut milk, well stirred

To Make the Cake

Preheat the oven to 350°F. Grease the bottom of a cake pan and line with parchment paper.

In a large mixing bowl, combine the butter and sugar and beat until light and fluffy with an electric handheld beater on medium-high speed, about 2 minutes. Add the eggs, one at a time, beating after each addition until well incorporated.

In a medium bowl, sift together the flour, cornstarch, baking soda, and salt. In a small bowl, whisk together the milk, yogurt, and vanilla extract.

Add about ⅓ of the flour mixture to the butter and egg mixture, beating until the flour is incorporated. Then add ⅓ of the milk mixture, beating until incorporated. Continue alternating additions, beating well after each addition, and ending with the flour mixture.

Pour the batter into the cake pan and bake for about 18 to 20 minutes, until the top of the cake is golden. Cool the cake completely before cutting. When the cake is cool, transfer to a cutting board. Cut ½ inch off the edges of the cake on each side. Score the cake 11 times lengthwise and 5 times widthwise to create a grid of even squares. Cut out the square with a serrated knife.

To Make the Coconut Icing

In a large bowl, whisk together the powdered sugar and coconut milk until it forms a thick frosting.

To frost the cakes, work with about 2 cups of frosting at a time. Dip each square of cake completely into the frosting. (Working with small batches of frosting minimizes the amount of crumbs in the frosting.) Place the individual cakes on a wire rack over aluminum foil, which will catch any dripping frosting. Drizzle a small amount of frosting on the top of the cakes as they rest on the wire rack. Top each cake with 3 gold dragées.

Transfer the cakes to the refrigerator for about an hour to allow the frosting to set. Remove the cakes from the wire rack and place in individual gold foil cups. Store in the refrigerator in a single layer until serving.

Pear and Apple Crumble

Serves 8

3 Anjou pears, peeled, cored, and sliced

2 Granny Smith apples, peeled, cored, and sliced

2 tablespoons lemon juice

½ cup almonds, ground

¼ teaspoon cinnamon

2 tablespoons brown sugar

2 tablespoons granulated sugar

½ cup whole wheat flour

4 tablespoons unsalted butter

Pinch of salt

Preheat the oven to 350°F. Combine the pears and apples in a mixing bowl, add the lemon juice, and stir to mix. Arrange the pears and apples in an 8x12-inch baking pan. Combine the almonds, cinnamon, brown sugar, granulated sugar, flour, butter, and salt in a food processor. Process until the mixture resembles coarse sand. Sprinkle the almond mixture over the pears and apples and bake for 40 minutes.

Peanut Butter Blondies
Serves 16

2 tablespoons peanut butter

Nonstick cooking spray

¼ cup canola oil

¾ cup brown sugar

1 large egg

1 teaspoon vanilla extract

1 cup ultragrain flour (or white whole wheat flour)

2 teaspoons ground cinnamon

⅓ cup semisweet chocolate chips

Preheat the oven to 350°F. In a microwave-safe bowl, heat the peanut butter in the microwave until runny, about 10 seconds. Set aside and allow to cool. Lightly spray an 8-inch square baking dish with nonstick cooking spray. Add the canola oil and brown sugar to the peanut butter and whisk until well mixed. Add the egg and vanilla extract and stir to blend. Add the flour and cinnamon to the peanut butter mixture and stir to combine. Add the chocolate chips and stir. Pour the batter into the prepared baking dish and bake for about 20 minutes, until a toothpick inserted into the center of the blondies comes out clean.

Chocolate Chip Cookies
Makes 24

½ cup butter

1 cup granulated sugar

1 cup brown sugar

2 eggs

2 teaspoons vanilla extract

1 teaspoon baking soda

2 teaspoons warm water

½ teaspoon salt

3 cups all-purpose flour

2 cups semisweet chocolate chips

Preheat the oven to 350°F. In a large mixing bowl, beat the butter and sugars until creamy. Add the eggs one at a time, beating well after each addition. Add the vanilla and stir. In a small bowl, combine the baking soda and hot water. Stir to dissolve and add to the sugar mixture. Add the flour and chocolate chips and stir until well combined. Drop by the spoonful onto a baking sheet, making sure the cookies are evenly spaced. You may need two baking sheets. Bake for 10 minutes, until golden brown.

Red Velvet Cupcakes
Makes 16 cupcakes

2⅓ cups cake flour (or 1¾ cups all-purpose flour plus 5 tablespoons cornstarch)

2 tablespoons cocoa

1 teaspoon baking soda

1 teaspoon baking powder

½ teaspoon salt

1 cup plus 1 tablespoon plain, low fat yogurt

1½ tablespoon red food coloring

1 teaspoon vanilla extract

1 teaspoon white vinegar

1½ cups granulated sugar

6 tablespoons unsalted butter, at room temperature

2 eggs, at room temperature

Preheat the oven to 350°F. In a medium bowl, sift together the flour, cocoa, baking soda, baking powder, and salt. Set aside. In a separate medium bowl, whisk together the yogurt, red food coloring, vanilla, and vinegar. Set aside.

In the medium bowl of a stand mixer (or using a handheld mixer), beat the sugar and butter on medium speed until light and fluffy. Add the eggs, one at a time, beating after each addition until well incorporated.

Add ⅓ of the dry ingredients to the mixing bowl. Beat on low speed. Scrape down the sides of the bowl, then increase the speed to medium and beat until all the ingredients are combined. Add ⅓ of the wet ingredients and mix until combined. Continue alternating additions of dry and wet ingredients, ending with the dry ingredients. Beat until smooth.

Place cupcake liners inside muffin pans and pour the batter into the pans. Bake for about 20 minutes, until a toothpick inserted into the middle of a cupcake comes out clean. Cool completely on wire racks before frosting.

Cream Cheese Frosting

¼ cup butter

1 8-ounce package ⅓ less fat Neufchatel cream cheese, at room
temperature

1 teaspoon vanilla extract

Powdered sugar (have at least 2 pounds)

In the large bowl of a stand mixer using the whisk attachment (or using a handheld mixer), beat the butter, cream cheese, and vanilla on medium-high speed until thoroughly combined. Add about 2 cups of powdered sugar and beat until well combined. Continue to add powdered sugar in 1-cup increments until the desired frosting consistency is reached. The frosting should form peaks but still be easy to spread. Use to frost cooled cupcakes.

Cookie Dough Bites
Makes 24

½ cup cashews or walnuts

½ cup rolled oats

½ cup graham crackers, crushed

3 tablespoons brown sugar

2 tablespoons maple syrup

⅓ cup peanut butter

1½ teaspoons vanilla

⅓ cup chocolate chips

Combine the nuts, oats, and graham crackers in the bowl of a food processor and process until powdery. Add the brown sugar, maple syrup, peanut butter, and vanilla and pulse to mix. Transfer to a bowl and stir in the chocolate chips. Roll into balls about ½ inch thick.

Caramelized Cinnamon Flan
Serves 6

½ cup granulated sugar

½ teaspoon ground cinnamon

3 eggs

1 egg white

1 cup fat-free milk

1 cup fat-free sweetened condensed milk

1 teaspoon vanilla extract

Preheat oven to 325°F. Lightly spray the inside of 6 6-ounce ramekins with cooking spray. Place the ramekins in a baking pan with tall sides.

In a small saucepan over medium heat, cook the sugar and the cinnamon. Continuously stir the mixture with a rubber spatula until the sugar becomes syrupy and is a light amber color. Turn off the heat. Working quickly, pour about a tablespoon of the sugar syrup into the bottom of each ramekin cup and tilt so that the syrup coats the bottom. Don't worry if the sugar starts to harden. It will re-melt during baking.

In a medium bowl, whisk together the eggs, milks, and vanilla until thoroughly combined. Ladle about ¾ cup egg mixture into each ramekin. Place the ramekins in the baking pan and pour water into the pan until it reaches halfway up the sides of the ramekins. Bake for about 40 minutes, until the custards set. Remove the ramekins from the baking pan and place in the refrigerator to cool, uncovered, for about 2 hours.

To serve, place a small plate on top of the ramekin. Flip both over so that the ramekin is on top of the plate. Wait for a few seconds, gently tapping the ramekin. The flan will eventually slip out.

Earl Grey Tea Cookies
Makes 36

1¼ cups all-purpose flour

¼ teaspoon salt

1½ teaspoons loose Earl Grey tea leaves

⅓ cup plus 1 tablespoon powdered sugar

7 tablespoons unsalted butter, diced and softened

1 tablespoon Earl Grey tea, brewed and cooled

In a small bowl, mix together the flour and salt and set aside. In a spice grinder, grind the loose tea leaves until coarsely ground. In a food processor, combine the powdered sugar, tea leaves, and butter. Pulse the mixture until the sugar and butter are well mixed. Add the flour mixture, and process until the dough starts to come together. Then drizzle with the brewed tea and process until all the ingredients are well combined.

Split the dough in half. Roll each half into a log about 1½ inches in diameter. Wrap each log in plastic wrap and place in the refrigerator for about 2 hours, or until cold.

Preheat the oven to 350°F. Slice the dough into ½-inch-thick rounds. Arrange on an ungreased, nonstick cookie sheet. Bake for about 12 minutes, or until slightly browned on the edges.

Pumpkin Pie with Gingersnap Crust

Serves 8

38 gingersnaps (about 5 cups), crushed

6 tablespoons unsalted butter, melted

1 15-ounce can puréed pumpkin

1 14-ounce can fat-free sweetened condensed milk

¼ cup maple syrup

2 large eggs

½ cup reduced fat milk

1 teaspoon vanilla extract

1½ teaspoons cinnamon

½ teaspoon ground ginger

½ teaspoon nutmeg

Preheat oven to 350°F. In a food processor, process the gingersnaps into crumbs. Drizzle in the butter and process until incorporated. Press the crumbs into a 9-inch springform pan until evenly distributed. Bake for 9 to 11 minutes.

In a large bowl, whisk together the pumpkin, condensed milk, maple syrup, eggs, milk, vanilla, cinnamon, ginger, and nutmeg. Pour the pumpkin mixture on top of the crust in the springform pan and bake for 58 to 60 minutes, until the center is mostly set. Cool on a wire rack for two hours, then cool completely in the refrigerator.

Pecan Pie

Serves 8

1 tablespoon water

2 teaspoons cornstarch

1¼ cups sugar

½ cup corn syrup

½ cup butter

3 eggs

½ teaspoon salt

1½ teaspoons vanilla

1½ cups pecans, chopped

1 9-inch unbaked pie shell

Combine the water and cornstarch in a small bowl. In a saucepan, combine the sugar, corn syrup, and butter. Bring to a boil over medium-high heat, then reduce the heat to medium and boil for 3 minutes, stirring frequently. Remove the mixture from the heat and allow to cool, about 15 minutes.

Meanwhile, preheat the oven to 350°F. Beat the eggs in a large bowl. Gradually add the cooled syrup mixture, stirring to combine. Add the salt, vanilla, and pecans and stir until thoroughly incorporated. Pour the mixture into the pie shell and bake for 50 minutes, or until set.

Note: For an adult pie, substitute 1 tablespoon bourbon for the vanilla and brush some bourbon on top after baking.

eighteen

Drinks

Sangria
Serves about 12

2 navel oranges, halved and sliced

3 black or red plums, halved, seeded, and sliced

2 apples, cored and diced

2 cups pitted cherries

1½ liters cabernet sauvignon (or your favorite red wine)

4 cups light cranberry pomegranate juice

1½ tablespoons orange blossom water (or Cointreau or Triple Sec)

2 cups club soda (or diet tonic water)

Combine all ingredients except the club soda in a large bowl and chill for about 4 hours. Before serving, stir in the club soda and add more juice to taste.

Hot Pink Kisses Champagne Cocktails
Serves about 15

1 pound strawberries, hulled and halved

2 cans lychee fruit in heavy syrup

3 to 4 tablespoons agave nectar

3 bottles (750 ml each) Rosé Brut Champagne (or any pink
   champagne), chilled

15 mint leaves

Place the strawberries in the bowl of a food processor. Add 1 cup of lychee syrup and the agave nectar and process until completely pureed. Place 2 tablespoons of the strawberry mixture in each of the 15 champagne glasses and top with champagne. Add 1 teaspoon of lychee syrup to each glass. Garnish each glass with a lychee fruit and a mint leaf.

Pomegranate Mimosas
Serves 9

¾ cup orange juice

1½ cups pomegranate juice (or light pomegranate juice)

2¼ cups champagne

Combine the orange juice, pomegranate juice, and champagne in a mixing bowl. Pour into champagne flutes and serve.

Raspberry Mojitos
Serves 1

6 mint leaves

6 raspberries

2 tablespoons sugar

1 shot of rum

Club soda

Muddle the mint leaves and raspberries with the sugar in the bottom of a glass. Add the rum and top off with enough club soda to fill the glass. Stir to combine. Add crushed ice if desired.

Ginger Beer
Serves 2

2 liters cold ginger ale

6 12-ounce bottles pale ale, like Sierra Nevada

Basil leaves

Combine the ginger ale and pale ale in a large punch bowl. Tear the basil leaves and sprinkle on top. Serve cold.

Cafe Sua Da

Serves 2

1¼ cups espresso

2 tablespoons condensed milk

¼ cup Kahlua

Whipped cream

Combine the espresso with the condensed milk and Kahlua. Top with whipped cream.

Kahlua Hot Chocolate
Serves 6

6 cups low fat milk

6 tablespoons Valrhona cocoa powder

6 tablespoons demerara sugar

¾ teaspoon cinnamon

1 cup Kahlua

Pinch of salt

In a medium saucepan over medium heat, combine the milk, cocoa powder, sugar, cinnamon, Kahlua, and salt. Whisk until the cocoa powder is completely dissolved. Serve hot.

Mudslides

Serves 2

¼ cup Kahlua

¼ cup Baileys Irish Cream

¼ cup vodka

¼ cup fat-free milk

1½ cups light vanilla ice cream

¾ cup crushed ice

½ teaspoon cinnamon

Combine the Kahlua, Baileys, vodka, milk, ice cream, ice, and cinnamon in a blender. Blend until frothy and serve immediately.

Spirited Green Tea
Serves 2

2 green tea bags

2 cups hot water

¼ cup lime juice

3 tablespoons sugar

¼ cup vodka

Steep the green tea bags in the hot water for 3 to 4 minutes. Add the lime juice, sugar, and vodka and stir until the sugar dissolves. Fill two tall glasses with ice. Pour and serve.

Basic Party Preparation Chart

Date	Task	Notes
2 weeks before	Shopping	Buy all nonfood items such as napkins, dinnerware, cutlery, decorations
1 week before	Shopping	Buy all drinks and nonperishable food items such as chips and crackers
3 days before	Shopping	Buy all perishable food items required by for recipes (e.g., ground beef, milk, sour cream, cream cheese)
2 days before	Cooking	Double-check ingredients and buy any last-minute items
1 day before	Set-up and cooking	Prepare dishes that will keep for a day, such as pinwheels, dips, cookies, brownies, or pies and set up tents, tables, and chairs
Day of the party	Decorating and cooking	

Vendors

Event Designers

Grand Soirées Event Design & Coordination (Birthday and Movie Night)

www.GrandSoirees.com

(949) 274-7725

Stylist: Linda Ly

Grand Soirées is an exclusive full-service event design and coordination firm. We create inimitable celebrations inspired by the lives and loves of our discerning clients.

Lovely Jubilee (Oktoberfest and Overnight Bash)

www.LovelyJubilee.com

(323) 412-0622

Stylist: Wilmarose Orlanes

Lovely Jubilee is an event design and styling studio that specializes in bringing stories to life and making memories of moments. We interweave the personal style of our clients with our innovative and whimsical designs to create unique events and picture-ready moments.

Sonia Sharma Events (Graduation and Bridal Shower)

www.SoniaEvents.com

(310) 802-9216

Stylist: Sonia Sharma

Sonia Sharma Events is one of the most sought-after special events companies on the West Coast. We specialize in high-end, multicultural events as well as an array of charity and corporate events, and are known for our unrivaled attention to detail and impeccable taste.

The Special Day (Cocktail and Engagement Party)
www.TheSpecialDay.net
(877) 731-2436
Stylist: Carolyn Chen
The Special Day is a full-service event planning and design company. We have been recognized for our planning and event management expertise and our inimitable design concepts. We place priority on providing clients with the most personalized experience.

DL/sh Design Studio & Utterly Engaged Magazine
(Housewarming and Tailgating)
www.DlshDesign.com
www.UtterlyEngaged.com
(714) 809-1106
Stylist: Lucia Dinh Pador & Henny Vallee
DL/sh Design Studio is a boutique brand experience design agency. Utterly Engaged is the first online Wedding and Bridal Magazine, and is devoted to inspiring brides with style. Thank you to our assistants: Lauren Marino, Samantha Aviles, Marcela Cebrowski, and Sara Kim.

Cakes and Specialty Foods

A Wish & A Whisk (Movie Night)
www.AWishAndAWhisk.com
(949) 648-3458
A Wish & A Whisk is a creative custom cake studio based in Costa Mesa, California, and specializes in edible works of art that taste as good as they look.

Chef Anahita (Housewarming and Tailgating)

www.ChefAnahita.com

(714) 343-3438

Stylist: Anahita Naderi

Chef Anahita Naderi specializes in a dynamic mélange of fresh ingredients, classical technique, and exotic flavors. She is accomplished in a wide variety of culinary styles to suit any occasion.

Delfin Jaranilla (Oktoberfest)

(562) 397-6397

Delfin Jaranilla's defines his cuisine as New American made with a French technique. He enjoys preparing rustic, cultural foods with a refined, modern twist. His motto: "Cook as if you're the one eating, and eat with all your senses!"

Sweet Gems (Birthday)

www.Sweet-Gems.com

(949) 981-5563

Sweet Gems is a two-time winner of the Food Network cake challenge. Based in Southern California, Sweet Gems specializes in wedding and special occasion cakes.

Special Cakes by Ruben (Bridal Shower)

(818) 523-1195

At Special Cakes by Ruben, we are famous for the beauty and originality of our cakes. We produce true works of cake art that create unforgettable memories catered specifically to your event.

Floral Design

Bloombox Designs (Bridal Shower)

www.BloomboxDesigns.com

(714) 685-1195

Bloombox is a high-end custom event design shop that believes that your event deserves to be transformed by a glamorous and elegant space.

Dolce Designs Studio (Engagement)

www.DolceDesignsStudio.com

(310) 684-2617

Dolce Designs Studio offers a wide variety of services, providing large scale, full-service event production as well as design for private, intimate celebrations. We value facilitating our clients' vision and creating the perfect environment for them.

Floral Sense (Birthday and Movie Night)

www.Floral-Sense.com

(714) 512-2443

Floral Sense is a sustainable floral and event design studio for extraordinary celebrations, committed to creating artful conceptions that reflect the couture design style of you.

The Flower Tray (Thanksgiving and Christmas)

www.TheFlowerTray.com

(909) 815-8283

Stylist: Tracey Go

The Flower Tray is a Southern California–based floral design studio devoted to making your event come to life through impeccable and elegant flower arrangements.

Nisie's Enchanted Florist (Cocktail)

www.NisiesEnchanted.com

(562) 596-7733

Enchanted Florist is one of Southern California's premiere floral studios specializing in the creation of unique, personalized weddings and special events. Our innovative floral designs are inspired by the personal style of our clients.

Hair and Make-Up Stylist

Muse Make-Up Artistry

www.MuseMakeupArtistry.com

(626) 383-0405

Our specialty is to accentuate every girl's natural beauty through makeup and hair design. From weddings to photo shoots to the runway, we do it all.

Invitations/Stationery and Graphic Designers

DL/sh Design Studio (Housewarming and Tailgating)

www.DlshDesign.com

(714) 809-1106

DL/sh Design Studio is a boutique brand experience design agency.

Felix Rhys Paperie (Birthday and Movie Night)

www.FelixRhysPaperie.com

(949) 607-8220

Felix Rhys Paperie specializes in custom letter pressed designs. Invitations, stationery, programs, and menus are just some of the items we produce by hand.

Invite Ink (Graduation)

www.InviteInk.com

(714) 747-7742

Invite Ink is well known for exquisite invitation designs made for a variety of events ranging from baby showers to graduations to weddings. Our goal is to revolutionize custom invitations using fine details, creativity, and superior workmanship.

Iris Media Design (Thanksgiving and Christmas)

www.IrisMediaDesign.com

(909) 569-2384

Iris Media was created with love by design and photography duo Carlene and Sonny Cruz. This husband and wife team works together in a wide variety of creative disciplines.

Papermade Design (Bridal Shower)

www.PapermadeDesign.com

Papermade Design creates custom event correspondence tailored to the client's event. Our invitations are printed on luxurious cotton paper with your choice of modern flat printing or traditional letterpress.

Jen Simpson Designs (Overnight Bash)

www.JenSimpsonDesign.com

(949) 614-9075

Jen Simpson Designs offers a team that strives to give you the best experience possible when you order invitations and paper goods for your special event.

Lighting and Projection

DJ Daisuke (Movie Night)

www.DJDaisEntertainment.com

(657) 464-3211

With over fifteen years of experience, DJ Dais delivers the best in state-of-the-art sound and lighting equipment, and also provides master of ceremony services and playlist customization.

Linens

Designer Specialty Linens (Birthday)

www.DesignerSpecialtyLinens.com

(310) 548-5183

Designer Specialty Linens has a wide range of fine linens, napkins, overlays, chiavari chairs, chair covers, and accessories that will enhance any decor. These items are available for rental or purchase.

Fusion Decor (Thanksgiving and Christmas)

www.FusionDecor.com

(949) 600-8851

The best selection of linens, furniture, specialty rentals, and fabric decor in Southern California.

Wildflower Linens (Bridal Shower)

www.WildflowerLinens.com

(714) 522-2777

Wildflower Linen offers designer table linen and chair cover rentals in styles ranging from fashion-forward to elegant and understated. Our linens have dressed Hollywood's most posh parties, elegant weddings, and banquets.

Rentals

Casa de Perrin (Housewarming, Tailgating, and Engagement)

www.CasaDePerrin.com

(310) 463-1652

Casa de Perrin is a full-service boutique rental company specializing in tabletop and decor. Our one-of-a-kind, bohemian, eclectic collections span continents, time periods, and design aesthetics.

Chiavari Chair Rentals (Engagement)

www.ChiavariChairRentals.com

(949) 480-1682

Chiavari Chair Rentals specializes in chiavari chairs, dance floors, tables, furniture, lighting, and draping for events of all sizes throughout Southern California.

Classic Party Rentals (Birthday, Movie Night, and Oktoberfest)

www.ClassicPartyRentals.com

(714) 540-6111

With more than twenty-five years of experience, Classic Party Rentals is the nation's leading full-service event rental company. We have numerous locations throughout the country.

Classic Party Rentals, Culver City (Graduation and Bridal Shower)

www.CulverCity.ClassicPartyRentals.com

(310) 202-0011 extension 111

Classic Party Rentals offers a deep inventory of tables, chairs, fine china, high-end flatware, specialty linens, centerpieces, tents, canopies, and more to our clientele.

Found (Housewarming and Tailgating)

www.Vintage-Rentals.com

(714) 888-5811

Found is an event decor and prop resource company supplying brides, event planners, designers, and photographers with unique vintage items to give their weddings, events, and photoshoots style and originality.

Lounge Appeal (Movie Night)

www.LoungeAppeal.com

1-888-229-9990

Lounge Appeal is a lounge furniture rental company ready to take your event to the next level. We rent high-quality lounge furniture for all types of special events.

Supplies

Franken Cutters (Birthday)

www.FrankenCutters.com/fc

We provide custom cookie cutters, cake pans, and more.

Leanna Lin's Wonderland

www.LeannaLin.com

(323) 550-1332

Leanna Lin showcases her eclectic handmade jewelry collection at *Leanna Lin's Wonderland!*, her shop in Los Angeles. Her designs are inspired by styles as varied as mid-century modern and Japanese pop culture.

Luna Bazaar (Birthday)

www.LunaBazaar.com

1-800-223-1106

Luna Bazaar specializes in paper lanterns, parasols, candleholders, and celebration decorations.

Midori (Birthday)

www.MidoriRibbon.com

1-800-659-3049

Midori offers an amazing selection of fabric ribbon and gift packaging.

Venues and Locations

Culver Hotel (Bridal Shower)

www.CulverHotel.com

(310) 558-9400

The Culver Hotel proudly opened its doors in 1924. Decades later, this beautiful landmark remains the jewel of downtown Culver City and a premier destination in Los Angeles.

Promenade & Gardens (Movie Night)

www.TurnipRose.com/promenade-and-gardens.htm

(714) 540-0500

Promenade & Gardens is a treelined haven nestled in the city. Run in partnership with Turnip Rose Catering, we are here to serve your special events needs with both indoor and outdoor facilities.

About the Authors

Ngoc Nguyen Lay is a born planner, dreamer, and achiever. She lives with her husband in Southern California, where she enjoys celebrations with family and friends on a regular basis. In 2005, she founded Skybox Event Productions (www.SkyboxEventProductions.com), a special event planning company that strives to provide every client with an unforgettable event, no matter what the occasion. Through Skybox Event Productions, Ngoc consistently seeks out new and innovative ways to share her event strategies and creativity with others.

Ngoc's writing has been published in magazines such as *Ceremony, Celeb Life,* and *Serendipity* as well as on several blogs. This is Ngoc's first book, and it was born from her passion to help others find inspiration for their events. Ngoc's dedication to celebration and festivity is grounded in a deep appreciation for the richness that family and friends bring to life. *Inspired Celebrations* aims to remind its readers that life is full of reasons to celebrate.

Tram Le is a registered dietitian and health food blogger. She runs Nutrition to Kitchen (www.NutritionToKitchen.com), a company dedicated to promoting healthy meals and raising funds for various charities. She believes that you can achieve a healthy, happy lifestyle by focusing on homemade dishes and ingredients grown from the earth. The recipes included in this book combine party foods with eating healthfully. Indulgent ingredients are used in moderation, and healthier substitutions are made when possible.

Tram has been published in *Audrey* and *Serendipity* magazines, as well as in the *ADA Times* (a publication of the Academy of Nutrition and Dietetics). She lives in Houston, Texas, with her husband and daughter. On her downtime, Tram can be found doing yoga, writing, and exercising.

Caroline Tran (www.CarolineTran.net) is a Los Angeles–based photographer who loves to travel and eat, preferably at the same time. She has photographed weddings in locations as far-flung as Hawaii, New York, and Thailand. Popular for her fresh, fashionable style, Caroline Tran's work can be seen in numerous publications both in print and online, such as *Destination Weddings*, *Ceremony*, *The Knot*, *Style Me Pretty*, and *Daily Candy*.

Caroline loves the relationships she forms with the people she photographs and appreciates the fact that her art allows her to participate in the milestones and intimate moments of her clients' lives. She believes there is no greater honor than to share in someone's joy by photographing their engagement, wedding, or growing family. Caroline's camera allows her to be her own boss, and her photography business has become a family affair. Her husband, Jonathan, is her business partner and second shooter, and their son often accompanies them on photo shoots.